PATHS TOWARD UT

Writing-speaking differently is part of the struggle for the world we want to create and are creating, a world that moves against-and-beyond capitalism. These picture-essay-poems break the existing world both in what they say and how they say it. A fabulous book; an honor to comment on it.
—John Holloway, author of *Crack Capitalism*

There is a haunting, fragile strength to the postapocalyptic images and texts that populate this book. They hover half in our world—punctuated by its many recent systemic failures—while they rend autochthonal longings from our bellies, as all good visionary imaginings of the future do, for a world seemingly as close at hand as the pages of the book that holds them.
—Brett Alton Bloom, artist/activist, Temporary Services

PATHS TOW

This remarkable book is inspiring and emboldening, allowing us to see the contours of another world that is not only possible but already in formation.
—Roxanne Dunbar-Ortiz, author of *Outlaw Woman: A Memoir of the War Years, 1960–1975*

A beautiful and meaningful book. Cindy Milstein and Erik Ruin offer us visions of a way out of the awful mess, and ways to think about *how* we might get out.
—Paul Buhle, editor of *Studs Terkel's Working: A Graphic Adaptation*

Paths toward Utopia avoids sweeping everything into a grand narrative; instead, multiple threads of radical possibility emerge from the daily actions that make up our ongoing practical responses to a world gone mad. Revolution is negation, sure, but it has to invite us all to move toward a better life too. In these drawings and words, an incipient agenda becomes visible, not as a future program to which all must adapt, but as a recognition that we are already, everyday, taking vital steps toward a radically transformed future.
—Chris Carlsson, author of *Nowtopia : How Pirate Programmers, Outlaw Bicyclists, and Vacant-Lot Gardeners Are Inventing the Future Today!*

The paths—wiggly and broken, unmapped, an adventure—are as important as utopia—somewhere distant. This book articulates part of that adventure. It tries to imagine not only what that unknown utopia might look like but also the beautiful pathways that will get us there. And the paths start right here, at our feet, on our laptops, in our hearts, and at the end of our street.
—Boff Whalley, Chumbawamba

These picture-stories are poignantly familiar; like the sweet pollen of a half-remembered tomorrow, carried on the breeze past our broken alleys and empty schoolyards. Milstein and Ruin urge us to take tools in hand, to prepare the hard dirt of vacant lots and battered hopes, transforming it into soils into which that loving, generous future can send out its roots. This book is itself a seed, an invitation to that bright world, rooted in our most authentic selves, to which we have never been but to which we long to return.
—Ricardo Levins Morales, artist/activist

ARD UTOPIA

GRAPHIC EXPLORATIONS OF EVERYDAY ANARCHISM

CINDY MILSTEIN & ERIK RUIN
FOREWORD BY JOSH MACPHEE

OAKLAND, CA

Paths toward Utopia: Graphic Explorations of Everyday Anarchism
Cindy Milstein and Erik Ruin

© 2012 PM Press

ISBN: 978-1-60486-502-8
Library of Congress Control Number: 2011917550

Cover design by Erik Ruin & Josh MacPhee
Interior design by Josh MacPhee/Antumbra Design

10 9 8 7 6 5 4 3 2 1

PM Press
PO Box 23912
Oakland, CA 94623
www.pmpress.org

Printed in the US.

CONTENTS

Acknowledgments   vii
Foreword by Josh MacPhee   ix
Prologue by Cindy Milstein   I

Solidarity Is a Pizza   I5
Good Defense   22
Food for Thought   29
What to Keep   32
Borrowing from the Library   42
Picking Up the Park   5I
Paths toward Utopia   58
The Gift   65
Deciding for Ourselves   74
Waking to Revolution   86

About the Contributors   I05

ACKNOWLEDGMENTS

Despite *Paths toward Utopia* being a collaborative effort between the two of us, we couldn't have done this book on our own. We're grateful to PM Press—namely, Craig O'Hara, Gregory Nipper, and Ramsey Kanaan—for taking this project and us seriously when there wasn't much proof that our fragmentary idea would coalesce into an embodied whole, and laboring hard to get it into print. Appreciation as well to all those who lent us their eloquent words in the form of blurbs, and before that, *World War 3 Illustrated* for publishing our first two picture-essays.

Crucially, Josh MacPhee has been one of our strongest advocates and most insightful critics—both invaluable gifts. He has also gifted us his words and design.

Last but not least, heaps and heaps of debt, of a thoroughly noncapitalist kind, to all the aspirations, flights of fancy, and working existences of the recent do-it-ourselves commons and movements from below—peopled by dreamers, agitators, occupiers, troublemakers and gender-troublers, critical thinkers, pirates, anarchists and autonomists, queers, rabble-rousers and rebels, and so many other misfits who haven't given up on themselves and each other, and are willing to be visionary vagabonds on this journey together.

Cindy   My greatest acknowledgment for this book is to Erik, as longtime dear friend and inspiration, as fellow heretic and, I trust, ongoing coconspirator. Josh MacPhee has stood by my side throughout, as another longtime dear friend and inspiration. If Erik and Josh both make me feel loved and at home in this inhospitable world, so too, always, does Joshua Stephens, and he yet again came to my mutual aid, training his keen mind and editorial eye on my prologue. Love also to utopias found during the development of these picture-essays—most poignantly, my Station 40 chosen family in San Francisco and my occupy neighborhood in Philly.

Erik   My deepest gratitude, of course, goes out to Cindy for going down this long road together with me, for struggling together to make the best that we could make, and for her patience and support. Thanks as well to my dear friend and constant inspiration Josh MacPhee along with the rest of my comrades in the Justseeds Artists' Cooperative. Nidal El-Khairy deserves kudos for his crucial assistance with Arabic-language slogans and signage in "Waking to Revolution." I'd also like to acknowledge Emmy Bright, Joshua Marcus, and Meredith Younger for feedback and advice at various stages.

FOREWORD Josh MacPhee

I hope the book you are reading is a turning point, a dawn in graphic politics. A writer and an artist have met in the space between their disciplines, and created something new. It is not a graphic novel in the traditional sense. Each chapter is more a poetic essay than a story driven by characters and narrative. It is not a series of illustrated essays either, for far too often the images drive the page, dismissing such a simple description of this work. What we have here is simultaneously a theoretical and graphic engagement with some of the most important ideas circulating in, and struggles facing, the world today.

At their best, Ruin's bold yet complex graphics lift Milstein's words, and together they successfully recast everyday political engagement as vital resistance and prefigurative transformation. His graphic renditions of Milstein's actual text always remind us that we write our own stories. The words emerge from mouths, shout from banners; they exist as graffiti on walls and words on homemade signage. Otherwise-dense theoretical frameworks become our words, thoughts, and conversations. In the integrated textual-image world Milstein and Ruin conjure, we glimpse a place where there is no longer a separation between thought and action, subject and object. We live our words. They are the walls we run into and the roads we walk along.

This is further captured by the compactness of word and image. These are not long essays we need to slog through. They are short and pithy, and read practically as action poems. Yet a cascade of ideas also flows within each one. It is the same with the imagery. A quick scan gives us the basic gist, but the overlays and reworkings invite us to dig deeper, to see exchanges and glances not held within the text alone.

The two-page chapter "Food for Thought" acts as a central pillar of the book. It solidly frames the different aspects of our survival under capitalism as both our doing and undoing. In Ruin's illustration, these acts and aspirations flood out of our mouths, turning our faces into both megaphones and broken fountains. Some of these (speech) acts buoy and nourish us. They are the water we drink, wash, and frolic in. But others we lose control over; they threaten to submerge us. This is the duality of our lives, illustrating the ways in which our survival techniques sustain us, yet paradoxically satiate the things we oppose. It is all water, and the struggle is how to drink without drowning.

The chapter "Solidarity Is a Pizza" brings out the subtleties of this dialectic—the ways that it works on us that we might not recognize. We are introduced to powerful and emotional examples of international solidarity, how simple gestures like an Egyptian worker ordering a pizza for occupiers in Madison, Wisconsin, become overwhelming symbols of the fragility of the borders that keep us apart. At the same time, in the final double-page spread, the crumbled border converts the basic equation of solidarity equals liberation into something more illusive. The wall has come down, but other boundaries remain. The two people sitting at the table across the once-existing border seem no closer, nor happier, than before. There are miles and decades of barriers, many invisible, between them that still need to be broken down. Here, graphic and textual representation work with and against each other, creating a richer fabric than either would do alone.

Paths toward Utopia continuously brings us back to the concept of the commons. The need for a commons, what we share among us with no claim to private ownership, is an idea so simple and powerful, yet simultaneously so elusive in the face of capitalism's ability to shape our perceptions of reality. The commons are often left hanging in the theoretical ether, seemingly just out of reach. By grounding them in our quotidian existence, our experience with public libraries ("Borrowing from the Library"), parks ("Picking Up the Park"), and gift giving ("The Gift")—activities that all readers will recognize—the commons become living things. We draw from and give to them; they nourish our actual lived lives, not merely the way we think about those lives. At the same time, while I revel in the common-sense-ness of these examples, part of me can't help but want to see the other sides too: the complications, poison gifts, and libraries that enclose rather than liberate knowledge. I'm not sure we can effectively build and protect our commons if we don't acknowledge their weaknesses and failings.

Overall there is a strong duality throughout the book—commons versus capitalism, surplus versus scarcity. This goes a long way toward allowing us to envision our lives as individual engines of utopian power. Our actions matter, and small steps can build toward bigger and greater leaps. But there are limits to this idea, to what we can do in our daily lives. Foregrounding our self-determination is dependent on just that: it comes from the self. As individuals, our resistance appears as little but a circus-mirror vision of the existing society we oppose. Are we but reactionary pawns responding, bending, and acting in response to capital, and not the other way around?

Thankfully, the poetic skeletons of liberation we glimpse in many of the short pieces here are given muscles and flesh by the longer and more detailed chapters that close the book. Focused on the social struggles in Argentina ("Deciding for Ourselves") and Egypt ("Waking to Revolution"), they show how self-determination can be about more than self. The grounding of the concepts of commons and autonomy, self-determination and self-organization, in these real-world examples of social struggle gives justification to the utopian impulse present throughout the book. We may not always see the underground currents of a different world. The economies we build to the side of capitalism may appear so small as to be insignificant. But the stories in this book give us glimpses of how to tend these precious sparks, lightly blow on them, and build them into a joyous bonfire.

Let this be an opening salvo, a call to artists and writers to attempt to break the bounds of their individual labors and collide, to spark the invention birthed by building together. Milstein and Ruin's collaboration was not seamless; the tension in their interactions can be seen in the work. This is where truly interesting things begin to happen, for isn't a call to utopia actually a call to drop our tools and pick up others, to become something else, something new?

Cindy Milstein

I remember reading Martin Buber's *Paths in Utopia* long ago, before I'd ever heard of one of the book's guiding lights, Gustav Landauer. It was before I'd visited the rebuilt-kitsch landscape of Munich, where Landauer had helped to make a revolution from below with his fellow anarchists nearly a century before, only to be murdered in the process, and where he now lies buried in that city's forever-bloodied soil. It was also before I'd lived in Europe for over two years, where I'd daily felt the ghosts not only of Landauer and other revolutionaries but so many "ordinary" people too—Jews, Roma, queers. They haunted my every footstep, whether I meandered past the sleek global architecture in Berlin being erected, literally, over Hitler's final bunker or walked along Treblinka's isolated dirt road crudely paved with pieces of broken Jewish tombstones, ransacked from cemeteries for this space of the final solution.

Landauer and his friend Buber's faith in "living and life-giving collaboration, an essential autonomous consociation of human beings, shaping and re-shaping itself from within," as Buber puts it, haunts *Paths in Utopia*, written in 1944, and to some degree, the work you now hold in your hands.[1] It's hard to imagine that anyone could still hang on to a concept of utopia in the mid-1940s, given that much of the world had become a graveyard. And it's just as difficult to understand how this pair of radical Jews and critical thinkers could find promise in the kibbutzim experiment, albeit its socialistic impulse—one of the paths in Buber's book—in the land that wasn't yet Israel but soon would become another kind of graveyard.

At the time, few saw much potential for the "renewal of society," to again cite Buber.[2] As another radical Jew and critical theorist, Theodor W. Adorno, famously observed in 1949, "Cultural criticism finds itself faced with the final stage of the dialectic of culture and barbarism. To write poetry after Auschwitz is barbaric. And this corrodes even the knowledge of why it has become impossible to write poetry today."[3] Nearly all was lost. Perhaps the best that could be hoped for was meticulously penning messages in a bottle, such as Adorno's, for future generations to find long after the wreckage of the twentieth century had sunk to the bottom of our collective experiences and memories.

Still, like a trash picker in a vast landfill, Buber set about the task of scavenging useful fragments in the here and now, from the given social reality, so as to "sketch the picture of an idea in process of development": utopia. For him, utopia was "the unfolding of the possibilities, latent in [hu]mankind's communal life, of a 'right' order." Buber's utopia at once sought "to stimulate" a "critical relationship to the present" in order to illustrate "perfection" as an ideal, but crucially, also had to serve "as something towards which an active path leads from the present." As he further explained, "We must be quite unromantic, and, living wholly in the present, out of the recalcitrant material of our day in history, fashion a true community."[4]

And now, in a different world altogether, although one exhibiting barbaric elements of neofascism in the United States and elsewhere, Erik Ruin and I heft aside more rubble so as to uncover paths of our own, but paths you can walk on too—or maybe already do. The switch to the preposition *toward* in our book's title is less a matter of splitting grammatical hairs—or avoiding outright plagiarism in our nod to Buber's book—than it is a substantive shift in how those of us fighting for individual and social freedoms see such transformation—revolution—happening. We harbor a far less messianic faith than Buber. Our preposition indicates that for us, like so many of our contemporaries, the road seems longer and fraught with more perils, offering faint probability of reaching a particular destination. Indeed, even as Erik and I seek directionality in behaviors and practices along with forms of self-organization close at hand, we're overly self-conscious about making any claims to an exit strategy from the resilient logic of domination. Or perhaps we're just a much more tempered bunch, healthily so, given that capitalism, to name one obvious foe, has only continued to extend its reach and recuperative powers over the decades. As Guy Debord contended in 1967, "The entire expanse of society is its portrait," and one could easily argue that this is truer now than ever before.[5] Utopian desires all too quickly become just another tempting commodity.

But if Buber, amid the dystopia of the 1940s, could proclaim that utopia, in Karl Marx's words, entailed people "consciously participating in the historical revolutionary process of society that was taking place before our eyes," then it behooves us to find cracks that we can further pry open in what seems like the smooth surface of social control.[6]

Halfway through creating our *Paths toward Utopia*, in fact, a yawning gap in history opened up: occupy everywhere.[7] Months before that other fissures appeared, from the creation of a do-it-ourselves city within a dictatorial one in Egypt to the directly democratic occupation of the Wisconsin State Capitol, and so many more. Each and every instance has shared several features, not least among them the element of surprise—with the participants perhaps being the most surprised of all. *The Coming Insurrection*'s counsel that a few like-minded radicals should "find each other," picked up as tinder for the "occupy everything" student movement in the United States a couple years ago, suddenly took on a substantively different meaning this past year.[8] People of dissimilar minds, and most far from radical, not only found each other by the hundreds and thousands in plazas, encampments, and assemblies worldwide in new face-to-face relationships; they also discovered and flexed their communal power-from-below, in all its startling beauty and messiness.

Erik and I kicked off our picture-essay making at a time when nothing seemed possible, well before the Arab Spring, by first testing our own creative relationship through pieces ("Paths toward Utopia" and "Food for Thought") for two issues of the graphic journal *World War 3 Illustrated*. We've finished this book amid the nervous anticipation of even more audacious uprisings globally this spring.[9] Throughout our collaboration of artistically "sketch[ing] the picture of an idea in process of development," we've balanced on the tightrope between the tension that marks any inching toward utopia, and that especially today, is stretched taut by the push-pull of utter despair and utter hopefulness. Almost by surprise to us, our book found its defining motif—the commons—inside this tension, precisely because it unfolded at this unanticipated yet wholly remarkable crossroads.

John Holloway states in his recent book *Crack Capitalism* that "the commons can be seen as the embryonic form of a new society: 'If the cell form of capitalism is the commodity, the cellular form of a society beyond capital is the common.' . . . If capital is a movement of enclosing, the commons are a disjointed common-ing, a moving in the opposite direction, a refusing of enclosure." He describes "an enclosure, an appropriation, [as] a separating of something from common enjoyment or use."[10] This can happen by privatizing land or anything else for that matter, including information, politics, caring, or the ecosystem.

A commons is a simple idea really, and something that humans have done throughout our existence, even before we had languages, even before we made up the word *commons* in multiple languages. It is the exact opposite of enclosure: something held by people in common, to be used, shared, and enjoyed. It can be a physical space, like a field for grazing or planting, or a library or park; knowledge, like the ideas within our libraries or free and open-source software; those things that sustain all of life, like the air and water; and what make us most human, such as empathy, imagination, and love. What all commons share is, precisely, a deep sense of sharing, in which our usage does not diminish the commons but rather increases its "worth" for everyone, and its worth is determined not by money or its exchange value but instead by how intrinsically useful it is to everyone. Like love, it only increases through our freely given shared use and enjoyment. We thus have a coequal interest in sustaining our commons. Much more than that, Buber maintains, "the real living together of [hu]man with [hu]man can only thrive where people have the real things of their common life in common."[11]

But besides commons as what we hold in common to use, enjoy, and share, there is the implicit and essential corollary: a commons is inherently something that we must self-manage and self-govern. If we share a field to graze our individual sheep on, each and every one of us knows that if one of us overgrazes their animals, the field won't sustain any of our sheep, so we'll need to figure out informal or formal ways to voluntarily manage our usage, enjoyment, and sharing such that the commons is sustainable and yet still commonly ours. Alongside collective management, though, a commons needs to be collectively governed. Again, implicit in the notion of something held in common is that we also all commonly have the ability to determine its use, enjoyment, and sharing along with the parameters around such activities.

Enclosure, then, goes well beyond denying us material sustenance; it also involves closing off possibilities and, critically, our power-together. In this way, the commons differs not only from privatization of all kinds but equally from anything dubbed public, including space, resources, or even the public good. There's always someone or something above "the public" that has the final say. Such ultimate power-over ensures that some humans—and in this era, fewer and fewer of them—will perpetually dominate not only the majority of humanity and even what it means to be human. They also will dominate the nonhuman world and what it means to supposedly be ecological. The commons instead intimately involves our collective power as caretakers to envision, decide, and implement a world in common, knitted together by a politics of dignity and solidarity. Holloway frames this notion as "the assertion, against a world that treats us as objects and denies our capacity to determine our own lives, that we are subjects capable and worthy of deciding for ourselves."[12]

This book's designer and author of the foreword, Josh MacPhee, was my guide, as it were, across the bridge of despondency toward the embankment of a commons looming, tantalizingly, so much closer than I could have ever dreamed. I happened to be in New York City this past September a couple days early for our twice-yearly meetings of the Institute for Anarchist Studies, of which Josh and I are both collective members, and Josh said, "You have to come see Occupy Wall Street!" He and his longtime partner, Dara Greenwald, were grappling with her near-imminent death from cancer, yet when Josh and I rendezvoused with her at a Brooklyn subway stop to travel to Zuccotti Park, I'd almost never seen either of them looking so alive. (Variations of the phase "I haven't felt this alive in years" would soon come to be echoed repeatedly to me during our own self-generated "beloved community" at the Occupy Philly encampment.[13] And Josh would later tell me, after the Wall Street and Philly occupations had both lost their physical spaces, and he and so many others had lost Dara, that Dara was drawn to Occupy Wall Street because it embodied a caring community—prefiguring a caring commons.)

Occupy Wall Street was a scant four days old, but Josh and Dara had already grasped its quirky import. Josh toured me around the outdoor occupation, from the concrete-bench-turned-library of a dozen or so mediocre books to the cigarette working group's table where several folks were busily rolling smokes, from a lone person silk screening T-shirts of his own design to the small group of MacBook users encircled into a tiny media area, to the two historical accidents that would so characterize this movement: the people's mic, because amplification was illegal, for increasingly large general assemblies, and an increasingly expansive mosaic of hand-painted cardboard signs, because there were so many discarded pizza boxes from the mountain of pie donations. Both the verbal sentence fragments and mass of eclectic written messages were near incomprehensible; misspeaks and misspellings abounded. When I asked person after person why they'd made their sign, using the instantly assembled materials in the on-the-ground art area, or why they had come to Zuccotti, they offered vague responses. They usually simply repeated their sign's slogan back at me, as if those words or images—which I could obviously just read or see—said it all. "Why the American flag?" I inquired of one hippie dude, who'd also drawn a smiley face, heart, and peace symbol on his creation. "The American flag," he answered, then added, with a look of wonder as to why I couldn't understand, "The American flag," followed after a pause by, "The American flag."

But like Josh and Dara, I recognized the power of this moment—like them, not fully, but enough. I was transfixed. Like Josh, I too became obsessed with the cardboard signage. For one, no one seemed to move any of the pizza-box placards once they were placed so reverently on the cold, hard pavement. And thus second, this crazy quilt (and it was overwhelmingly crazy—crazy incoherent, but also crazy homophobic, crazy racist, and so on) of signs kept spiraling outward, while huge crowds of strangers mingled on its edges to engage in animated though often-incoherent conversations.[14] When at one point I tiptoed between the pieces of cardboard to take photos, alarmed voices backed up by gesticulating arms warned me to step out of what clearly was seen by most not as a corporate-owned and police-protected private plaza, or a public one, but a sacred space, a commons. This commons, in turn, was making visible its participants' deepest intuition that something in the world was terribly, terribly wrong and that somehow, here, they'd be able to figure out together how to make the world, a new world, terribly, terribly right. That was about as much as anyone could articulate, but it was enough.

In a generational moment when, up until Occupy Wall Street, *community* frequently meant the disembodied aloneness of social networking via Facebook, Twitter, Tumblr, texts, and cell phones, or a thoroughgoing estrangement from the world, this occupy commons was all about the power of embodying one's "status update" among so many others, and having those others "find each other"—be able to directly look each other in the eye, listen, respond, dialogue. Time and time again, those at Zuccotti, usually completely new to politics or apolitical, kept saying, "You don't understand how incredible it is to be here with everyone else." As the working groups started to click, as Occupy Wall Street hammered out its "Declaration of the Occupation of New York City" using an intriguing mix of directly democratic debate along with paper drafts posted near the people's library for hundreds to scrawl comments on, thereby aiding in redrafting followed by more debate and amendment before its affirmation, as this occupation in the symbolic heart of global capital sent shock waves around the world and aspirational lifeblood to other cities to do their own takeovers and tent cities, it increasingly hit me just how deeply capitalism had damaged the majority (or that way too uncritically defined 99 percent) and created a shared sense of suffering (the truth, on the other hand, that's encapsulated in the 99 percent slogan)—enough that face-to-face communities felt, and alas are, novel.[15] Or enough that, well, "enough is enough," ya basta!

Particularly in this space called the United States, where "our" very origin story elevates the entrepreneurial individual, where the "American dream" is about pulling oneself up by one's own bootstraps, where every home foreclosure or imprisonment is seen as a personal failure, the near-overnight shift in sensibility from private, nuclear relations to common, collective ones was astonishingly utopian in itself. What I didn't understand at first was how powerful it actually was for many, many people to simply find each other—in person. Self-organization and self-governance was almost an accidental by-product of the desire to stay put with this spontaneous beloved community, so qualitatively different than anything most of those people in Zuccotti, and soon other cities and small towns, had ever experienced and literally lived within before. If everyone wanted to stick together in this newfound "family" (another word that would be repeated ad nauseam initially, but given substance as our contingently assembled family began to learn how to get along in all our startling beauty and messiness, through thick and thin, consensually), by necessity we had to provide ourselves with everything we needed, or everything for everyone, because anyone could enter the space of occupy.[16] We had to set about becoming, unexpectedly and without a map, do-it-ourselves cities within cities, with us occupiers as part do-it-ourselves city self-managers and part do-it-ourselves camp counselors.

In this increasingly difficult process of constructing a new world completely in the belly of the beast—in civic spaces that we never thought we'd be able to hang on to for so long—it wasn't merely that we created a friendship or chosen kinship commons. We became new selves as we stumbled awkwardly about the implicitly anticapitalist business of trying to forge a new society. Within the daily space of occupy, the speed at which people re-created or rather undid themselves to shed decades of socialization by structures like patriarchy and racism was dizzying, and that continues still, even without our encampments. Within this book, this dialectic of self-societal transformation is hinted at, for example, in our picture-essay "Waking to Revolution." It's not fast enough for many, of course. But each time I've personally been just on the verge of giving up, metaphorically, on humanity or myself, an occupier or two—or several, or even my whole general assembly—surprises me with the giant steps they've made in their ethics, politics, and behaviors, thereby also reshaping this occupy microsociety of ours, and I in turn surprise myself at how I've changed.

That first day that Josh took me to Occupy Wall Street, we kicked into anarchist self-organizing mode, perhaps falling back a little too comfortably on what we know how to do best: educate and agitate, with the aim of getting people to think and act for themselves. We decided to gather up some good radical books to add to the then-miniscule library and started tossing around ideas for some posters. Josh honed in on the image of the Wall Street bull's buttocks, and I crafted the trio "commons not capitalism."[17] He used the backside of the bull for other posters, and a couple weeks later, I picked up my phrase for a painted banner to help launch my "home" occupation in Philly, where I'd coincidentally just moved. Like my collaboration with Erik on this book, though, our common musings allowed for more than any individual brainstorm. Indeed, I keep coming back to how we and so many others knew almost without knowing from the get-go that occupy represented a grand contestation, challenge, and invention of a new commons—out of and against a world that has become enclosed in more ways than the heart or a smiley face can bear any longer.

From Cairo to Madison, from Athens to New York, from Barcelona to Oakland, on the shoulders of Chiapas, Seattle, and Buenos Aires, in "Asia's unknown uprisings" along with occupies, de-occupies, and unoccupies urban and rural, and in so many crevices in between, we the billions have joyfully, startlingly, raced to the window on history that's been flung open.[18] We are a product of this historical moment certainly, yet globally, perhaps in a way never before seen in the story of humanity, we're busily making history, doing history. It may not be inevitable, but quite likely this window on history will slam shut again, fiercely and just as suddenly. So it's imperative that we quickly though intentionally beat it as far down as many paths toward utopia as we can before it closes, (re)appropriating as many commons not enclosures as we're able to imagine and annex.

In this uneven process, we may find that our rebellious reconfigurations are actually leading us toward what Michel Foucault calls "heterotopias." He ruminates that "there might be a sort of mixed, joint experience" between utopias ("fundamentally unreal spaces") and heterotopias ("real places . . . something like counter-sites, a kind of effectively enacted utopia in which the real sites, all the other real sites that can be found within the culture, are simultaneously represented, contested, and inverted"): the mirror. "Starting from this gaze that is, as it were, directed toward me, from the ground of this virtual space that is on the other side of the glass, I come back toward myself; I begin again to direct my eyes toward myself and to reconstitute myself there where I am." Yet for Foucault, like our perspective here in this book, we're more likely to remain always on a journey, in a queasy "floating piece of space": the boat. A boat is "closed in on itself and at the same time is given over to the infinity of the sea"; it is at once "the great instrument of economic [colonial] development" and "simultaneously the greatest reserve of the imagination. The ship is the heterotopia par excellence. In civilizations without boats, dreams dry up, espionage takes the place of adventure, and the police take the place of pirates."[19]

In my case, trying to move from what can only be an exilic existence under the contemporary social structure into the uncharted territory of a new society all too frequently entails part alienation, part depression, and part mess. I know that I'm breathing the fresh air of utopia, however, when I occasionally feel at home in the world, and the process of this book with Erik has always held that euphoric quality. Not that it was always fun. In fact, fun is probably not the first word that would spring to either of our minds. It's been work—not merely the work that writing on my own or making art on Erik's own takes but rather the exponentially more difficult task of meeting within the "no-man's-land" of language and image. *Paths toward Utopia* really was and is a collaborative project, and yet we found again and again that much as we're both committed to such an ethos, it's difficult to navigate. The intersectional commons where our respective artistic sensibilities converged and conversed was precisely where the hard work came in, because that dynamic space points beyond the present, and it's tough thinking past the hegemony of this particular period. So at times it felt like we had run aground in a heavy fog.

Still, in my mind's eye, I keep seeing the image of Dorothy, the Scarecrow, the Tin Woodsman, and the Lion in the *Wizard of Oz* film as they emerge from a poppy field to see the glorious Emerald City ahead, rushing toward its beauty. Of course, once there, the glisten quickly tarnishes, yet collectively they push forward to newfound realizations. At the movie's end, when Dorothy gets back to Kansas, she insists that her quest "wasn't a dream. It was a place. And you—and you—and you— and you were there," and then marvels, "There's no place like home." In my reading of this film, hers is not a return to sameness, in the same old physical house, though. She and those around her, via their tempestuous travels, have become more than they were before by discovering what the good witch Glinda tells Dorothy toward the finale: she "always had the power" to transform herself and her community, but "she had to learn it for herself." Moreover, because of this, she is now embedded—literally waking up in her bed, surrounded by her closest companions—in "no place," the etymological meaning of utopia, which now feels "like home."[20]

I feel as if Erik and I, while creating this book, have been wandering along a similar yellow brick road, desirous of unearthing potential no places within the deadening spaces of today. But what we hadn't counted on was that at the end of our own arduous journey, we also landed somewhere unexpected. Our individual arts—words and images—by engaging in a reciprocal dialogue within the "creative commons" of our picture-essays, together invented a new language that somehow spoke to us, helping each of us to find new "power" within ourselves. I'm not sure how it happened—whether as Foucault's metaphoric mirror or boat, or both—but our collaboration facilitated an enriching of our own artistic styles over this past year or so, and thus our own selves and how we engage in wider communal efforts. Perhaps that sense, for me, of our process as one of making and remaking heterotopias isn't as invisible on these pages as I think it is; perhaps it shines through our poetic portraits.

Toward the end of finishing this book, Erik wanted me to write some fragments on occupy for a picture-essay articulating the flights of exuberance that marked its early days. Try as I might, I couldn't personally step out of the idea that hasn't yet been evicted—whether occupy maintains or retakes physical spaces, or finds its power in the political, ethical, or existential space of its expanding diasporic communities sans encampments—to get enough distance to fulfill Erik's wish.[21] The idea has not yet run its course, even if many of us occupiers are suffering from wintery bleakness before what I hope is a blossoming of occupy again this spring, and into the summer and beyond. In this accelerated instance of traversing the battered byway toward utopia, it's too hard to peer ahead at exactly where we're going and hence it's difficult to speculate on it in print.

I trust, however, as does Erik, that you'll catch glimpses of the breathtaking prefigurative heights of occupy and other people power movements within several of our picture-essays. For example, "Deciding for Ourselves" supplies a narrative of magical realism that flits across time and space, borrowing from some of the highs of low moments, such as the neighborhood assemblies and self-managed factories springing out of Argentina's financial collapse in 2001, the Common Ground Health Clinic in the wake of Hurricane Katrina in 2005, and some of the deeply human interconnections and processes that have been facilitated by occupy. Yet much more than these peaks, we encourage you to savor the calmer saunters through daily routines that point toward qualitatively better lives—lives worth living.

Which brings me to this book's subtitle: *Graphic Explorations of Everyday Anarchism*. Its double entendre within the word everyday—as in "daily" and "routine," or "ordinary"—aims to grasp, subtly, the double-edge quality of this quieter search for rocky yet promising footholds out of our present-day quagmire.

A good chunk of our picture-essays look at those things that many of us do now, in our daily lives, that model not an anarchist world—that is, one in which everyone must subscribe to one particular political orientation—but rather an anarchistic one—namely, one of our own making and doing, often within spaces that we can increasingly transform into commons. We try to capture this in such pieces as "Picking Up the Park" and "Good Defense," which draw out the power of self-activity, whether for leisure or necessity. In "The Gift," we unpack this almost-unthinking social obligation as perhaps affording a route beyond capitalism, in the same way that Francis Fox Piven recently highlighted the power of the lived experimental practices within occupy of a "moral economy" against the deadening "immoral economy" of the current market system.[22]

Yet this book is also intended to supply hints of what it routinely would be like to live, every day, in a nonhierarchical society, moving from a world premised on the social organization called neoliberalism and capitalism, say, to one looking a whole lot more like that advocated by anarchism: a freely self-organized society of freely self-determining individuals. What if, in other words, beloved communities from below replaced top-down structures that remove us from lives worth living? What if they were the norm of our social relations and social organization, something that was the common sense of our daily lives in common(s), both unremarkable and ordinary, rather than the exception? We offer glimmers of this movement "from here to there" in "What to Keep," which repurposes a current object of much protest—the bank—into something we might be able to use, enjoy, and share. You'll see glances as well in "Borrowing from the Library," which further widens the already-expansive supposition by bell hooks that "one of the most subversive institutions in the United States is the public library."[23]

The binding of "the community-forms that remain" in the present and "a new spirit" in the future is, we assert in this book, only to be uncovered and discovered in the tension created in the gap of those hierarchies and forms of domination that send us careening off the path of social transformation, only to resiliently and bravely venture forth again. We will find and experience utopia not in some definitive end but rather, as Buber writes, in our "bold but precarious attempts to bring the idea into reality."[24]

Paths toward Utopia is thus not a rosy-eyed stroll through potential commons, toward some fixed and forever-defined freedom. The book tries to retain the bittersweetness of present-day efforts to "model" horizontal institutions and relationships of mutual aid under increasingly vertical, exploitative, and alienated conditions. It tries to walk the line between potholes and promise. Yet if autonomous, do-it-ourselves efforts are to serve as a clarion call for more innovative actions, they must illuminate how we qualitatively, consensually, and ecologically shape our needs as well as desires. They must offer stepping-stones toward emancipation—an emancipation that will then continually renew itself. This can only happen through ongoing experimentation, by us all, with diverse forms of self-determination and self-governance, even if riddled with contradictions in this contemporary moment—in every moment. As the title piece to this book steadfastly declares, serendipitously reverberating Buber's sentiment above, "The precarious passage itself is our road map to a liberatory society."

NOTES

1. Martin Buber, *Paths in Utopia* (1944; repr., Syracuse, NY: Syracuse University Press, 1996), 14.
2. Ibid., foreword.
3. Theodor W. Adorno, "Cultural Criticism and Society" (1949), in *Prisms* (Cambridge, MA: MIT Press, 1981), 34.
4. Buber, *Paths in Utopia*, foreword, 8, 15.
5. Guy Debord, *Society of the Spectacle* (1967; repr., Detroit: Black & Red, 1983), para. 50.
6. Buber, *Paths in Utopia*, 2.
7. Which in turn, through the opening created by occupy but also in the necessary criticisms of it, has exponentially amplified calls for as well as grassroots organizing efforts to unoccupy and de-occupy many places.

8. The Invisible Committee, *The Coming Insurrection* (Los Angeles: Semiotext[e], 2009), 97.

9. By way of illustrating just how surprising this moment is—and how excruciating it feels to put any thoughts on it to paper—since I penned this prologue over two months ago, a student strike in Quebec and especially Montreal has grown into a maple spring of grand proportions. And this week, as it celebrated its hundred-day anniversary on May 22 and thirty days of nightly street demonstrations, this already-enormous movement has escalated into a widespread social strike, or maple summer—just to point to one of the many current twists and turns.

10. John Holloway, *Crack Capitalism* (London: Pluto Press, 2010), 29–30.

11. Buber, *Paths in Utopia*, 15.

12. Holloway, *Crack Capitalism*, 39.

13. For a sense of the occupy commons and the life it generated, see my "Occupation in Philly, Day 20 (October 25): Commons Not Capitalism," *Outside the Circle* blog, http://cbmilstein. wordpress.com/2011/10/26/occupation-in-philly-day-19-october-24/ (accessed March 9, 2012). Martin Luther King Jr. ("Nonviolence: The Only Road to Freedom," *Ebony*, October 1966, 30) popularized the notion of a beloved community with his often-cited observation, "Our goal is to create a beloved community and this will require a qualitative change in our souls as well as a quantitative change in our lives." In his book *Growing a Beloved Community* (Boston: Skinner House Books, 2004, xiii), Tom Owen-Towle contends that in the early 1900s, U.S. philosopher Josiah Royce first used the phrase in print, and it was picked up in visions such as that of Clarence Skinner, a Universalist minister, who argued that to create a beloved community on earth, we must embark on "the task of inventing and applying arts which shall win all over to unity, and which shall overcome their original hatefulness by the gracious love, not of mere individuality, but of communities." For bell hooks ("A Revolution of Values: The Promise of Multi-Cultural Change," *Journal of the Midwest Modern Language Association* 26, no. 1 [1993]: 10), a beloved community also necessitates that "we must stand for justice, have recognition for difference without attaching difference to privilege."

14. I'm aware that the word *crazy* can feel like, or even be, an insult in relation to mental health/wellness, and how the pharmaceutical-industrial complex's medical model in particular and society at large in general both stigmatize those it categorizes as mentally ill. Here I'm harkening to the Icarus Project: "We recognize that we all live in a crazy world, and believe that sensitivities, visions, and inspirations are not necessarily symptoms of illness," and more specifically, that we currently live "in a world gone mad," in which, in my view, the sane are crazy, and those labeled crazy are frequently the most brilliantly perceptive. See Icarus Project, "Mission Statement," http://theicarusproject.net/about-us/icarus-project-mission-statement (accessed March 7, 2012), and "You Are Not Alone Sticker," http://theicarusproject. net/product/youarenotalonesticker (accessed March 7, 2012).

15. New York City General Assembly, "Declaration of the Occupation of New York City," #OccupyWallStreet, September 29, 2011, http://www.nycga.net/resources/declaration/ (accessed March 13, 2012).

16. Which isn't meant to minimize how hard it was and is for many people to enter and stay in the physical, political, or psychic space of occupy—an ongoing process of how unity in our diversity looks in our experimental moment of attempting to create beloved communities from below.

17. See http://occuprint.org/Posters/CommonsNotCapitalism (accessed March 9, 2012).

18. So many good people's histories could be cited here, but since it uncovers some of the least-seen rebellions, at least among North Americans and Europeans, see George Katsiaficas, *Asia's Unknown Uprisings, Volume 1: South Korean Social Movements in the 20th Century*, and *Volume 2: People Power in the Philippines, Burma, Tibet, China, Taiwan, Bangladesh, Nepal, Thailand, and Indonesia, 1947–2009* (Oakland, CA: PM Press, 2012).

19. Michel Foucault, "Of Other Spaces" (1967), *Architecture/Mouvement/Continuité* (October 1984), http://foucault.info/documents/heteroTopia/foucault.heteroTopia.en.html (accessed March 9, 2012).

20. *Wizard of Oz*, 1939, movie script by Noel Langley, Florence Ryerson, and Edgar Allen Woolf, based on book by L. Frank Baum, sfy.ru/?script=wizard_of_ox_1939 (accessed March 14, 2012).

21. See Occupy Wall Street, "You Can't Evict an Idea Whose Time Has Come," September 15, 2011, 1:36 a.m. EST, http://occupywallst.org/article/you-cant-evict-idea-whose-time-has-come/ (accessed March 7, 2012). Thanks to Rabbi Arthur Waskow of the Shalom Center for the notion of a diasporic occupation community—or the search for one—in the aftermath of our evictions. For my tentative thoughts on various present-day moments, such as my recent "May Day Matters" piece, see my *Outside the Circle* blog, http://cbmilstein.wordpress.com/.

22. See Francis Fox Piven, "The Movement for a Moral Economy," *Al Jazeera English*, November 14, 2011, http://www.aljazeera.com/indepth/opinion/2011/11/2011117132329620899.html (accessed March 9, 2012). See also E. P. Thompson, "The Moral Economy of the English Crowd in the Eighteenth Century," *Past and Present* 50 (1971): 76–136, http://libcom.org/history/moral-economy-english-crowd-eighteenth-century-epthompson; Murray Bookchin, "Market Economy or Moral Economy?" in *The Modern Crisis* (Montreal: Black Rose Books, 1987), 77–98.

23. bell hooks, *Rock My Soul: Black People and Self-Esteem* (New York: Atria, 2003), 95.

24. Buber, *Paths in Utopia*, 14–15, foreword.

SOLIDARITY IS A PIZZA

IT'S AN EGYPTIAN WORKER IN CAIRO ORDERING A PIZZA,

FROM A PIZZERIA IN WISCONSIN

TO FEED ANOTHER WORKER IN MADISON,

PROTESTING ATTACKS ON COLLECTIVE BARGAINING.

SOLIDARITY

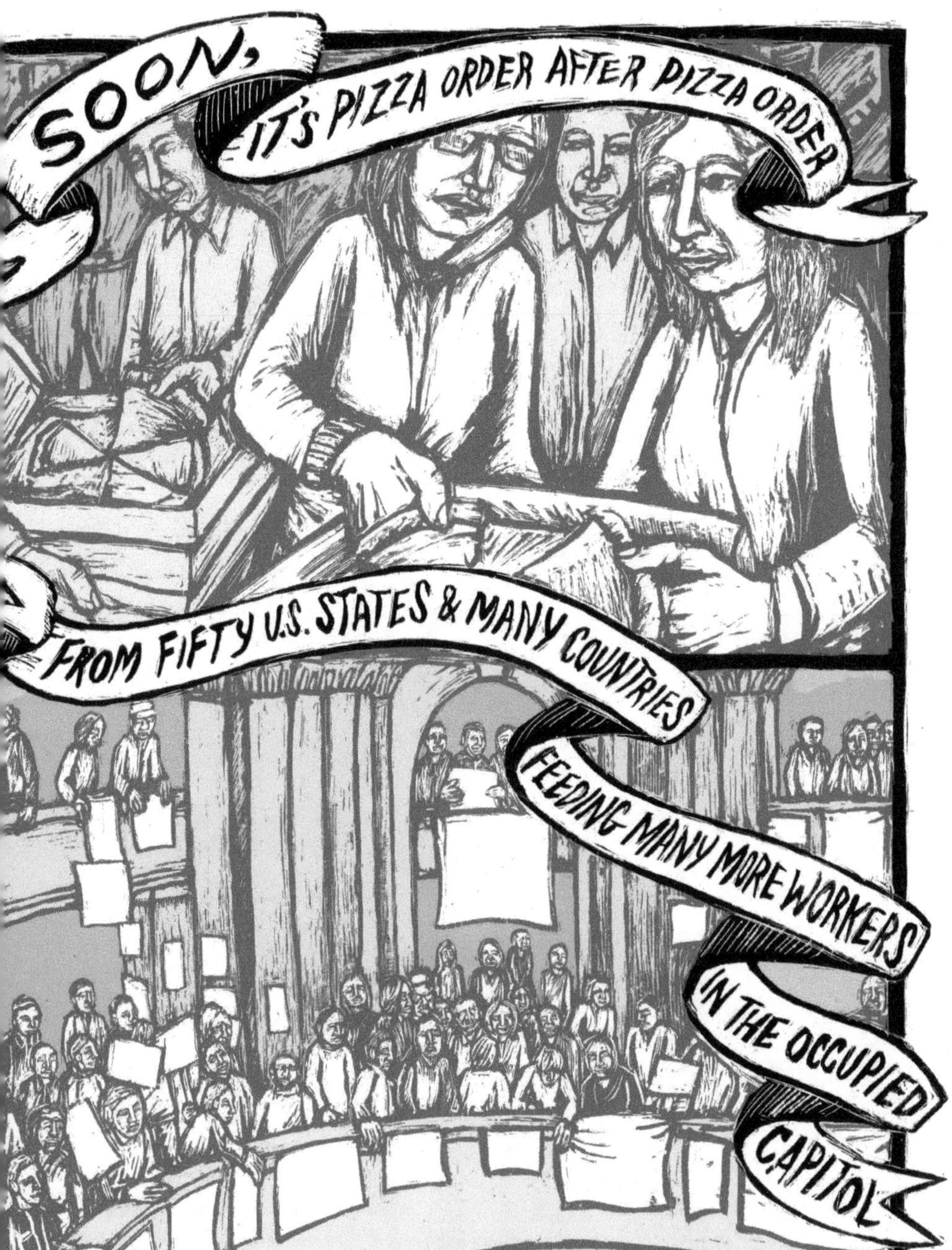
SOON,
IT'S PIZZA ORDER AFTER PIZZA ORDER
FROM FIFTY U.S. STATES & MANY COUNTRIES
FEEDING MANY MORE WORKERS
IN THE OCCUPIED
CAPITOL

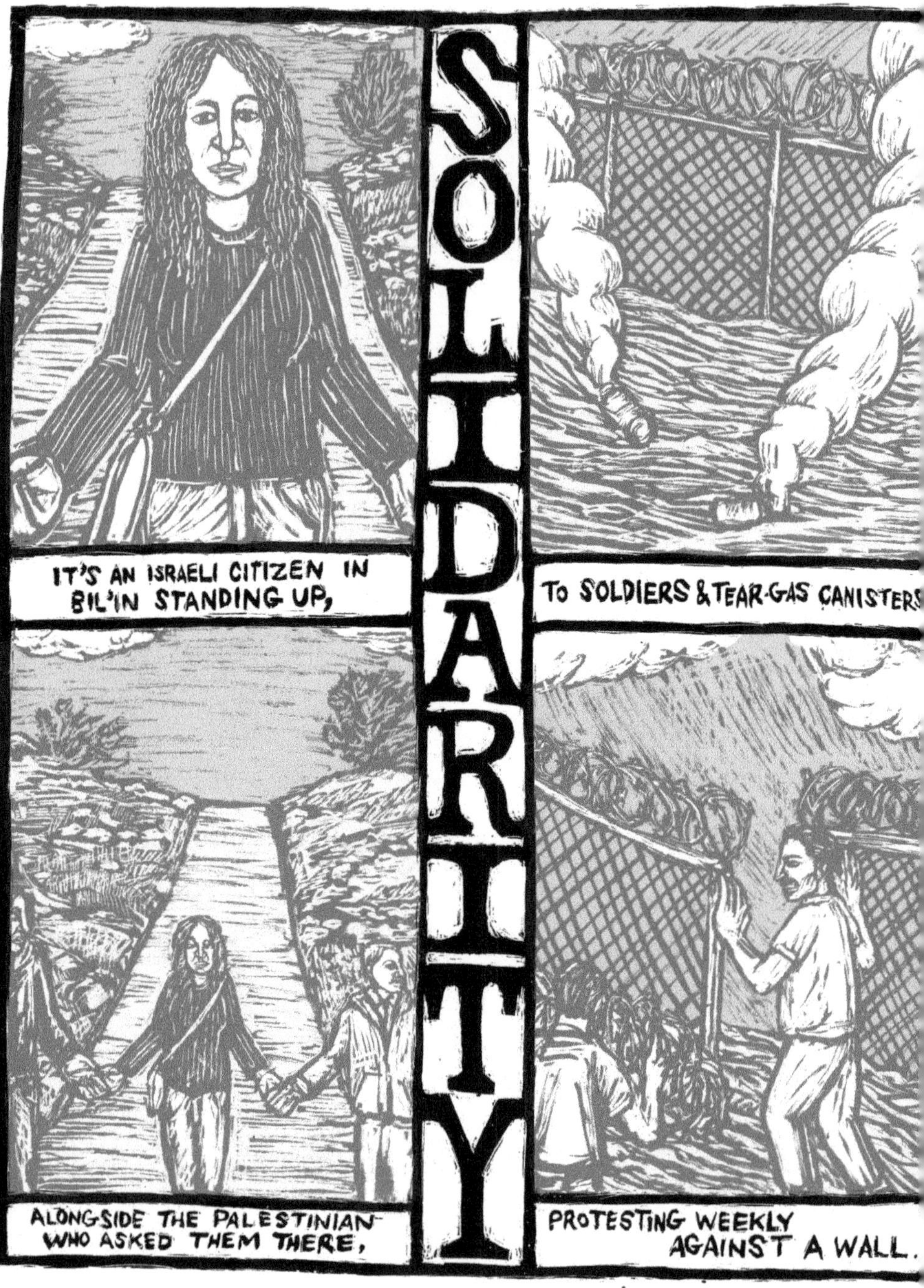
SOLIDARITY
IT'S AN ISRAELI CITIZEN IN BIL'IN STANDING UP,
ALONGSIDE THE PALESTINIAN WHO ASKED THEM THERE,
TO SOLDIERS & TEAR-GAS CANISTERS
PROTESTING WEEKLY AGAINST A WALL.

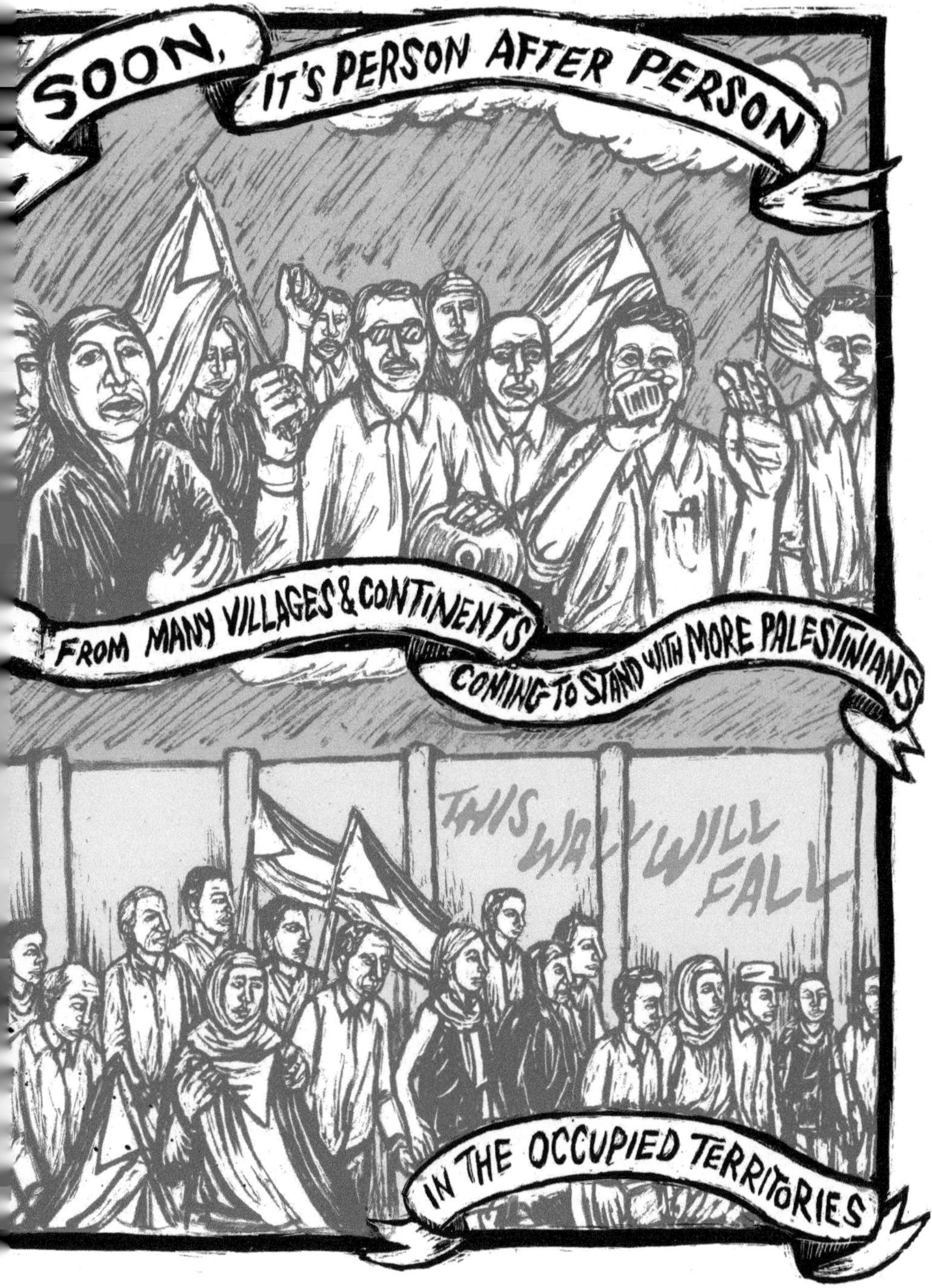
SOON, IT'S PERSON AFTER PERSON
FROM MANY VILLAGES & CONTINENTS
COMING TO STAND WITH MORE PALESTINIANS
THIS WALL WILL FALL
IN THE OCCUPIED TERRITORIES

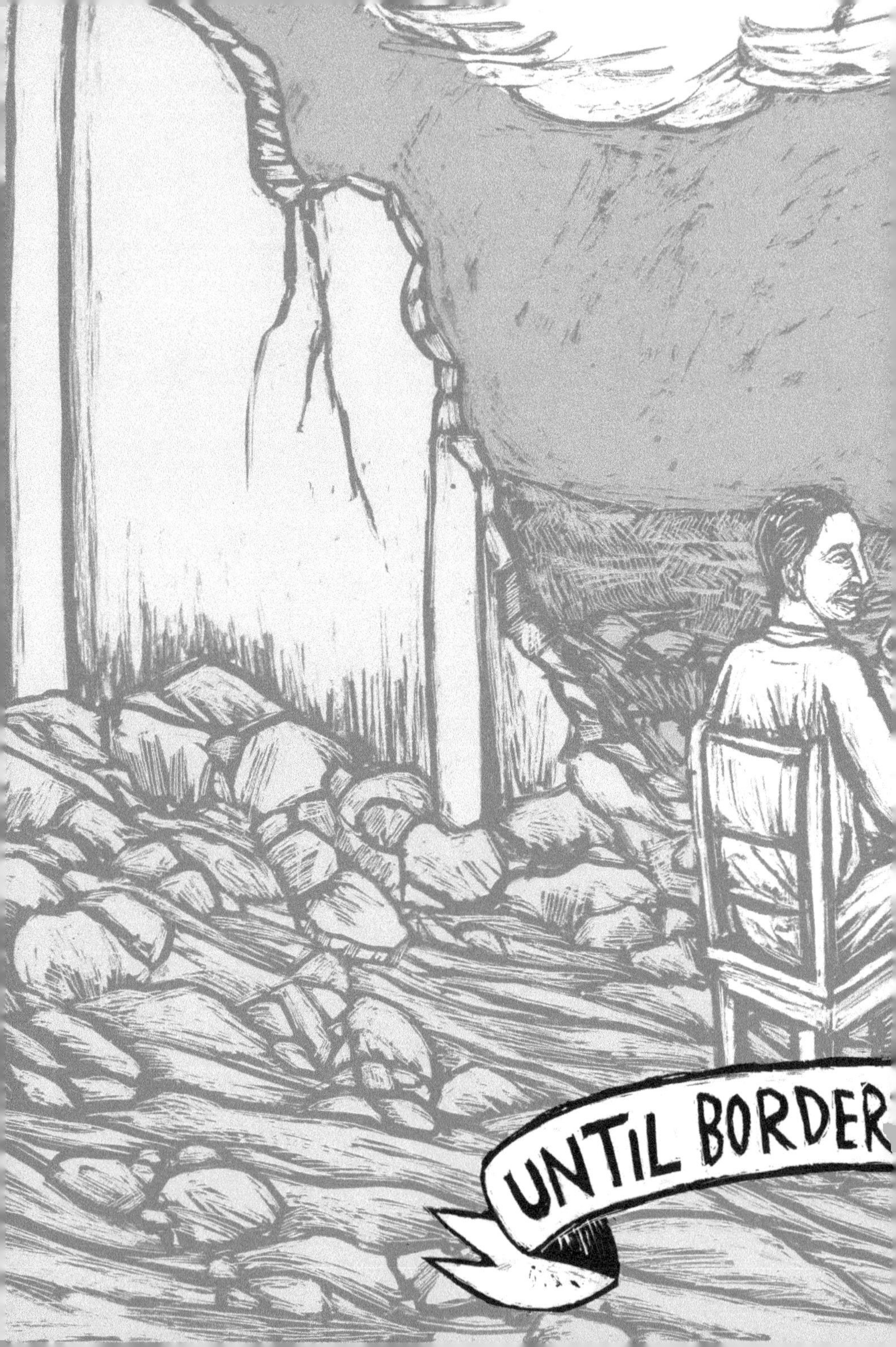
UNTIL BORDER

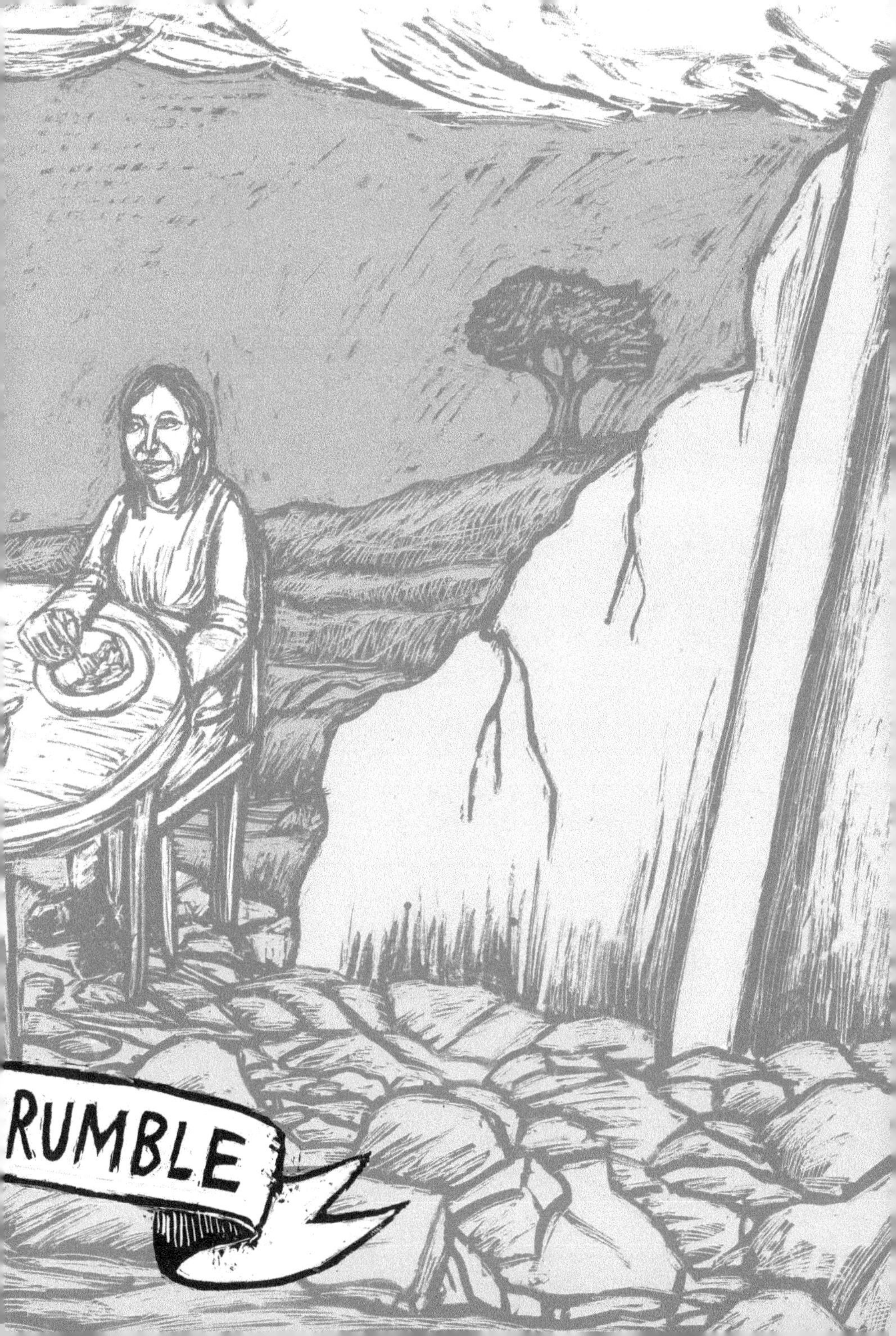
RUMBLE

GOOD DEFENSE

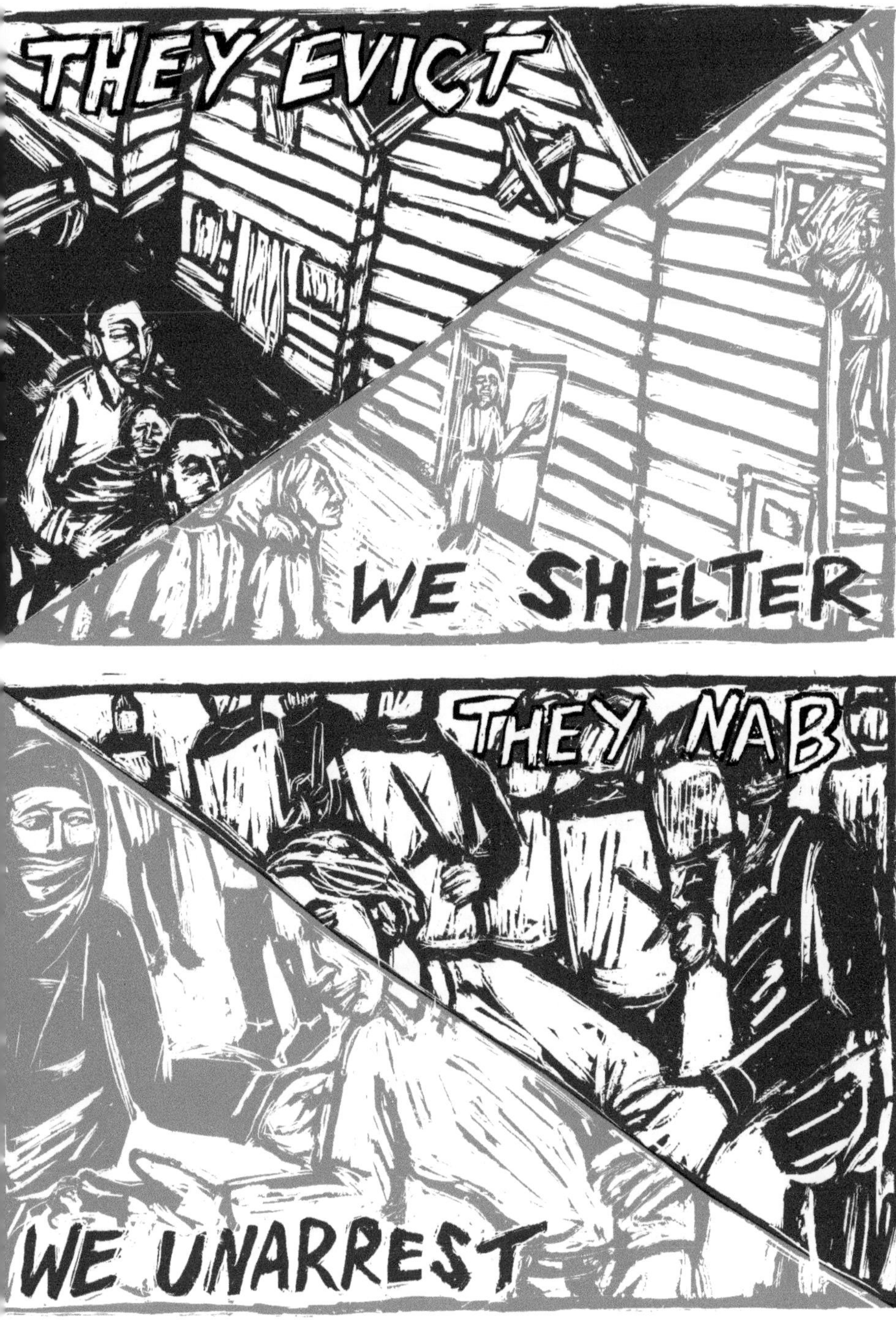
THEY EVICT
WE SHELTER
THEY NAB
WE UNARREST

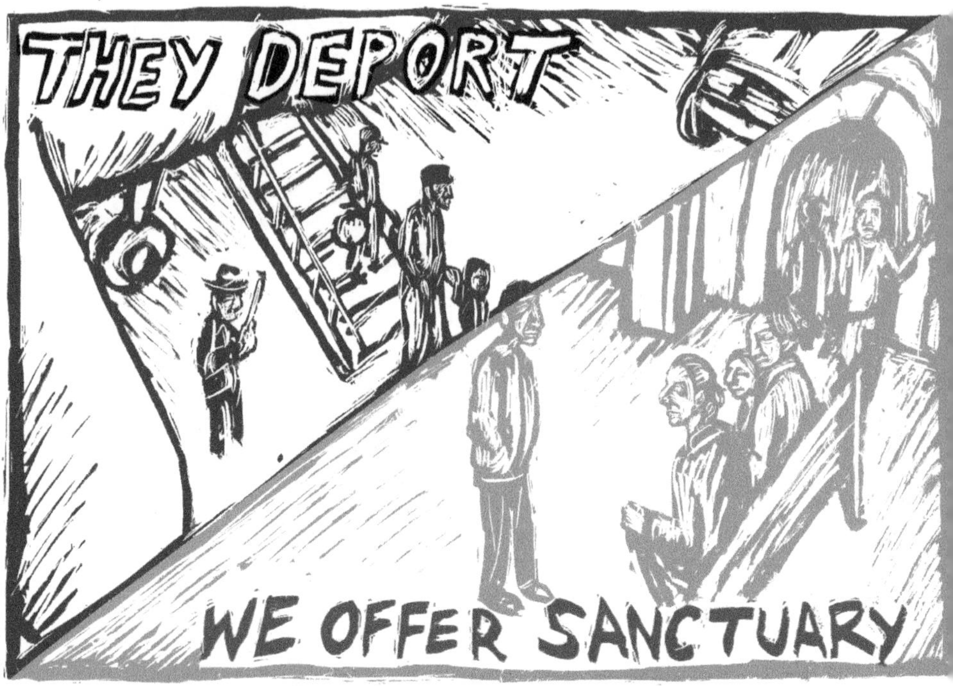
THEY DEPORT
WE OFFER SANCTUARY

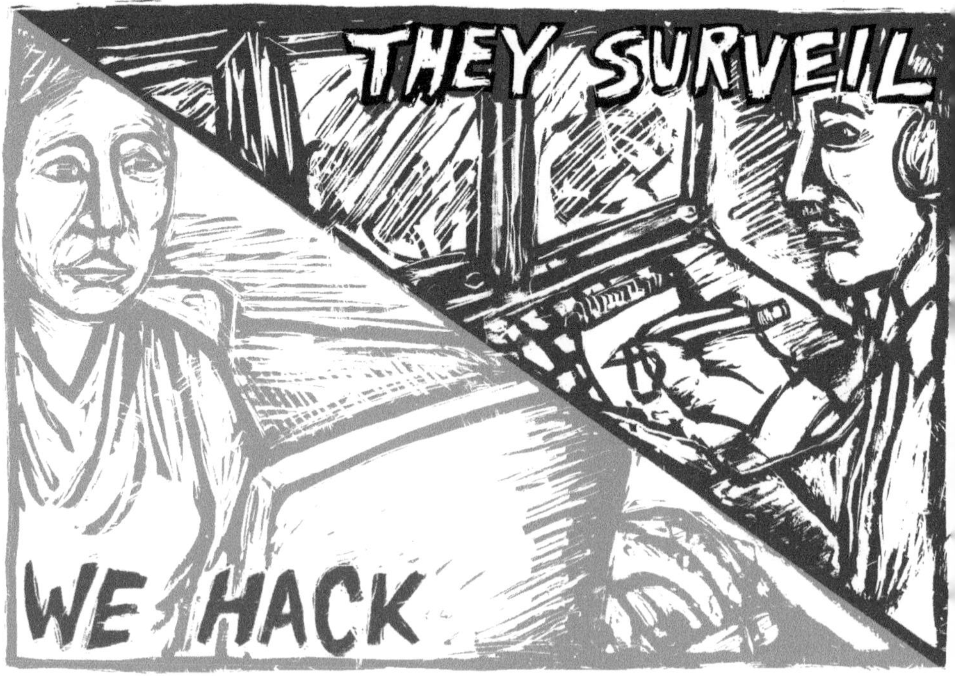
THEY SURVEIL
WE HACK

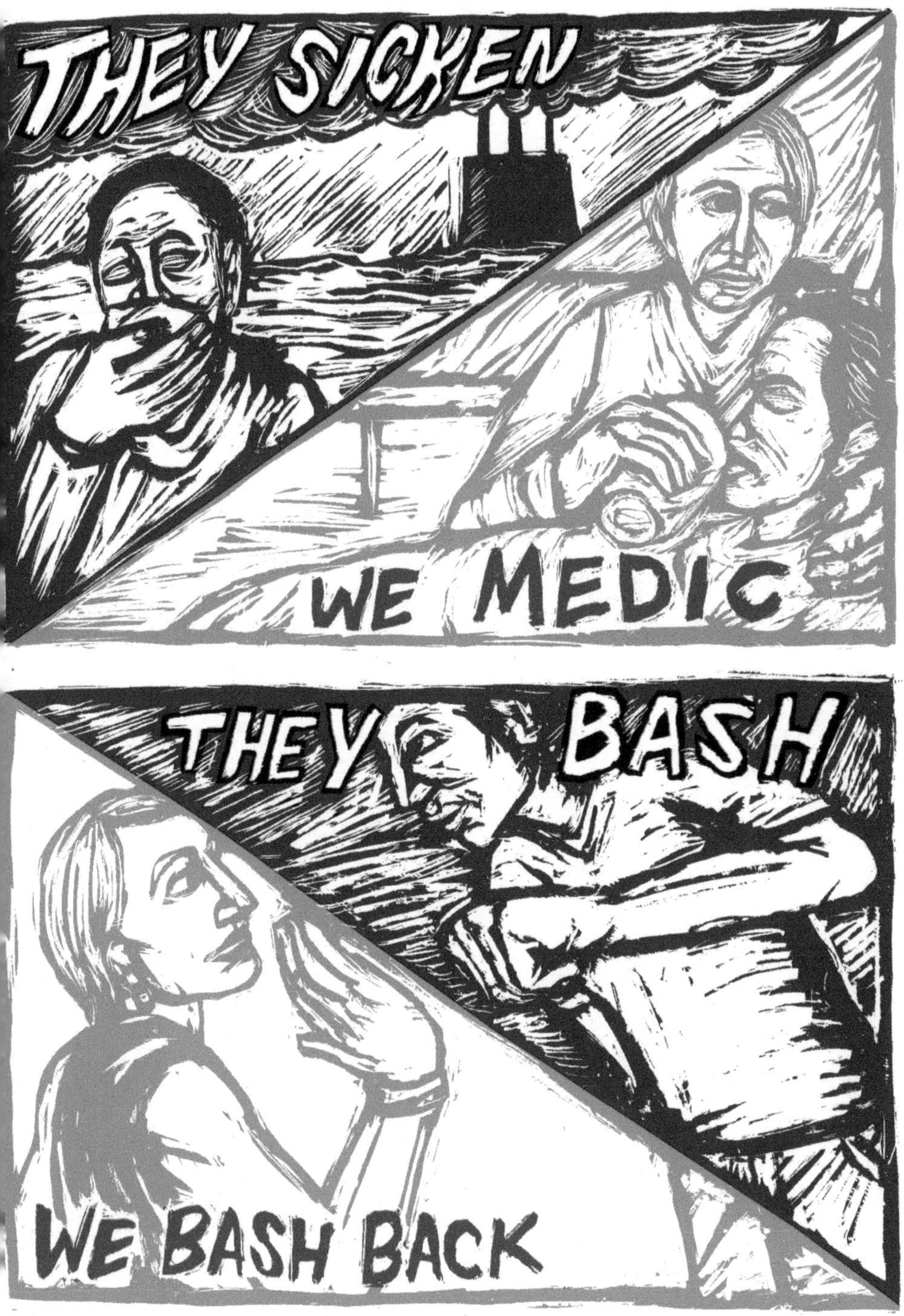
THEY SICKEN
WE MEDIC
THEY BASH
WE BASH BACK

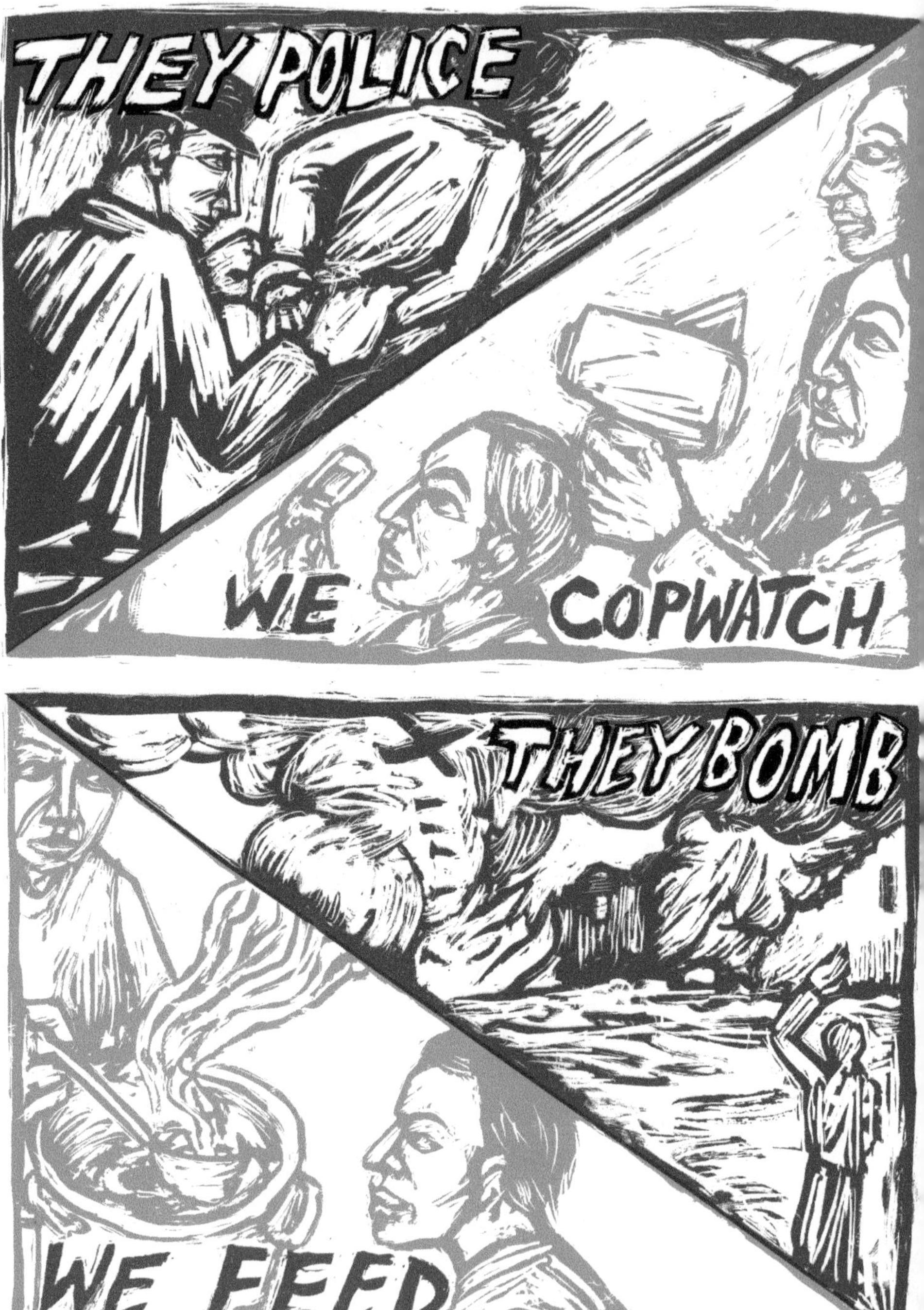
THEY POLICE
WE COPWATCH
THEY BOMB
WE FEED

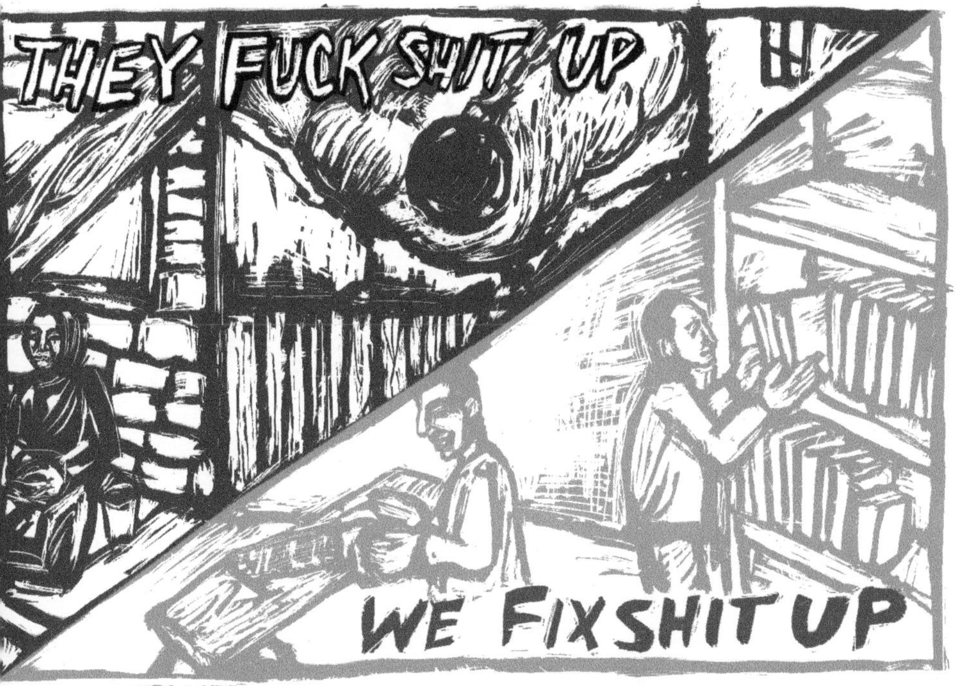
THEY FUCK SHIT UP
WE FIXSHIT UP

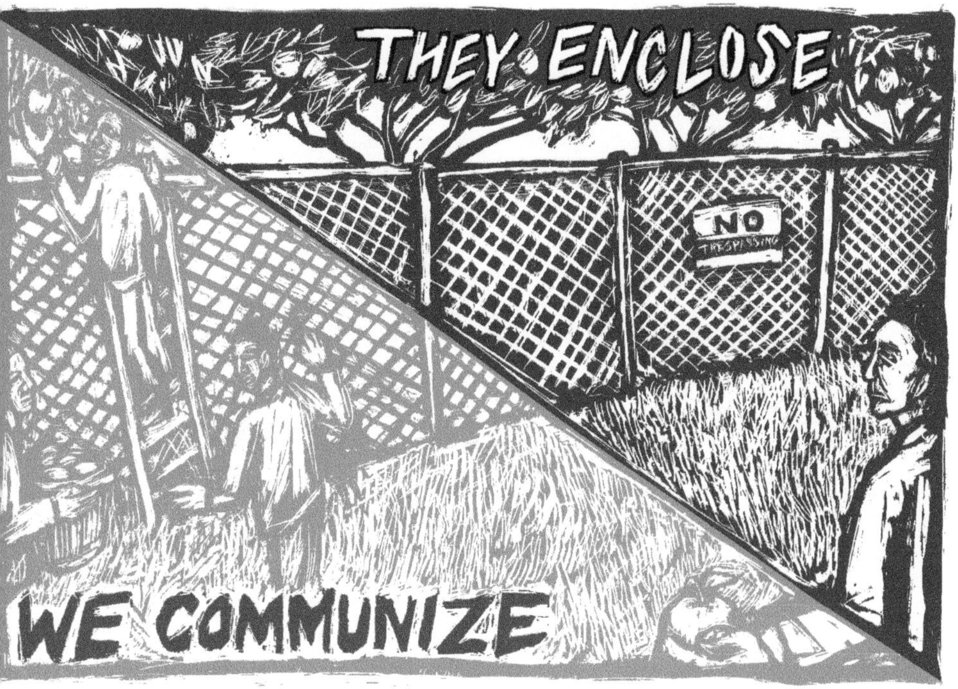
THEY ENCLOSE
NO TRESPASSING
WE COMMUNIZE

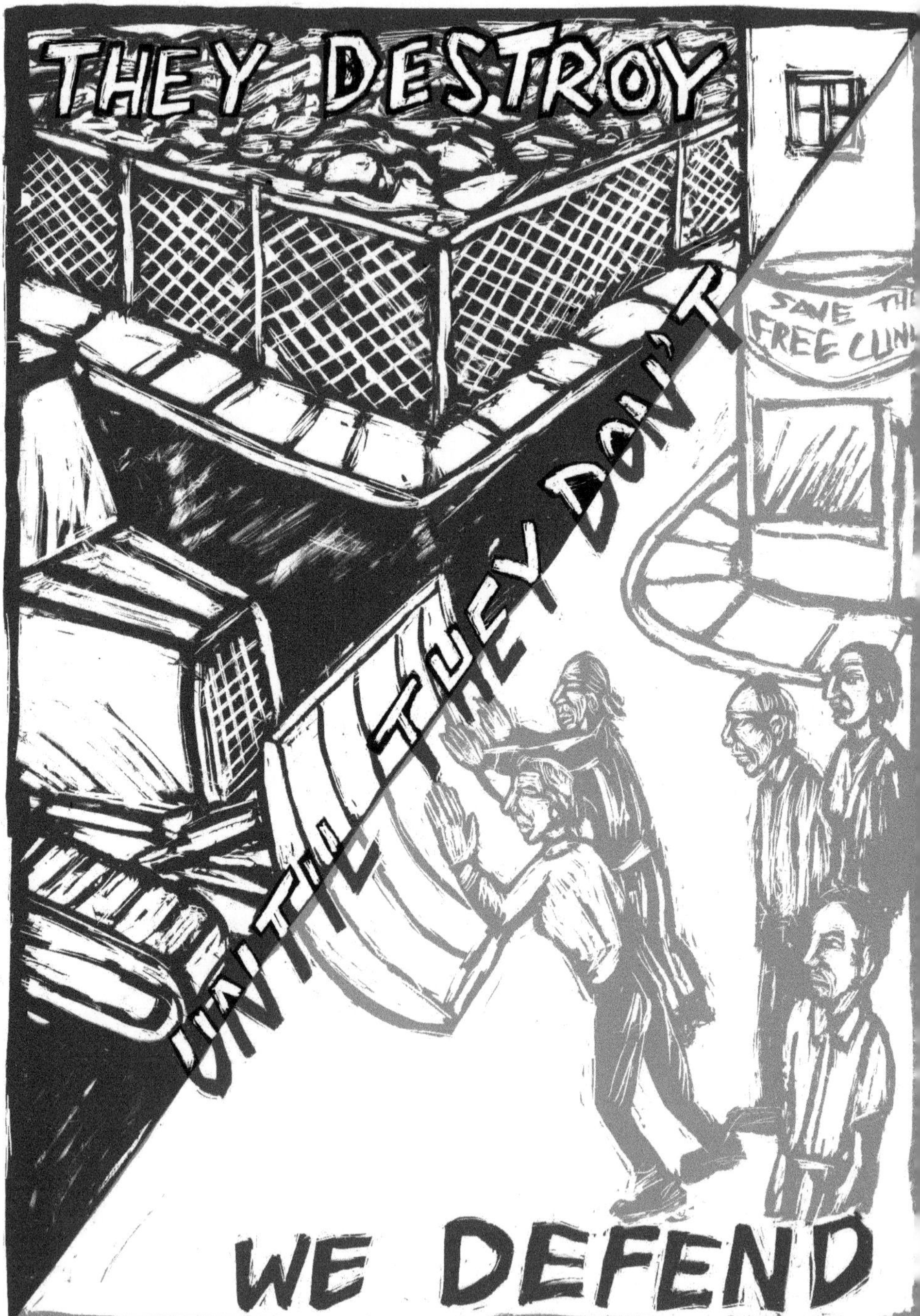
THEY DESTROY
UNTIL THEY DON'T
SAVE THE FREE CLINIC
WE DEFEND

FOOD FOR THOUGHT

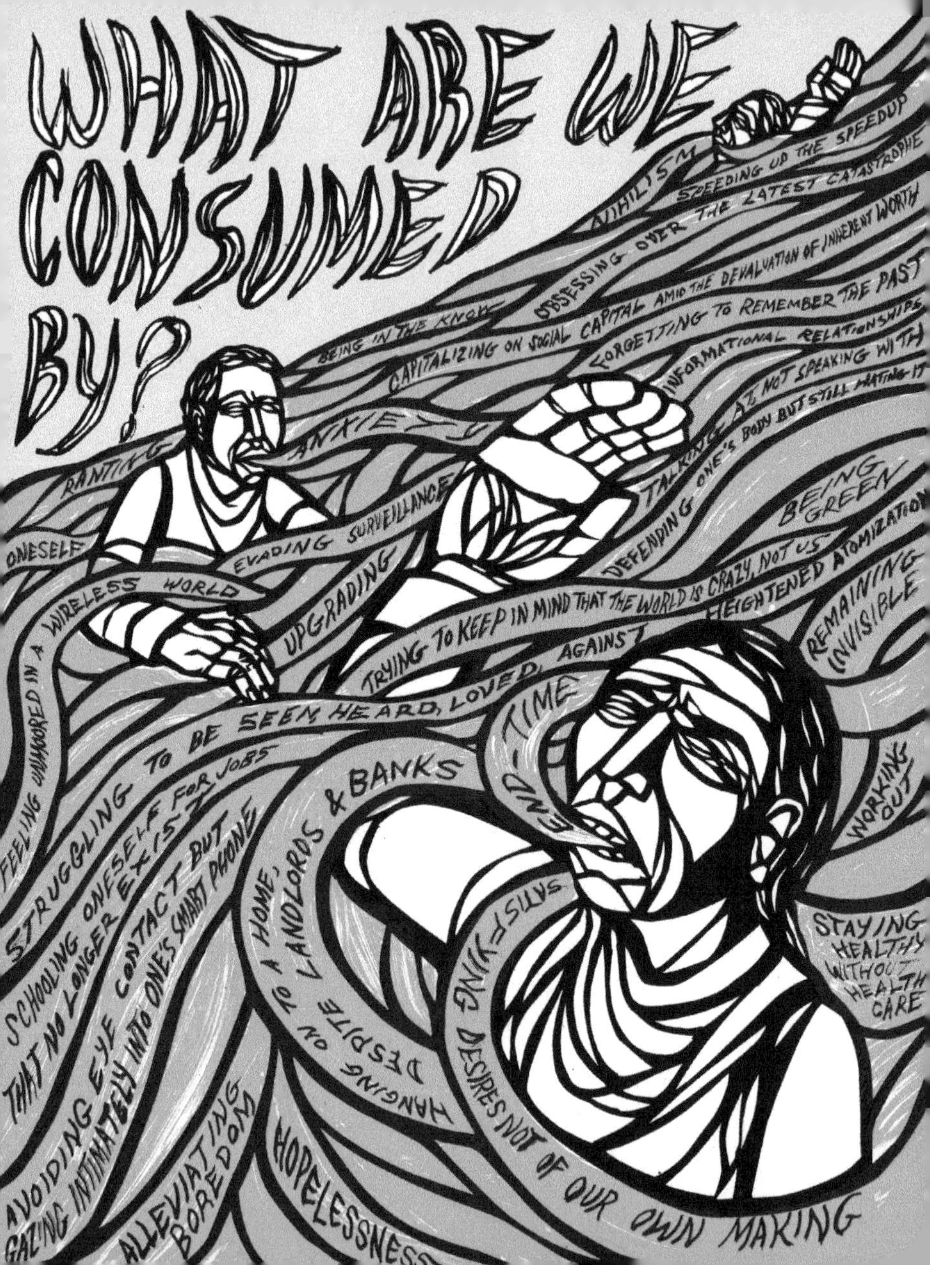
WHAT ARE WE CONSUMED BY?
NIHILISM
SPEEDING UP THE SPEEDUP
OBSESSING OVER THE LATEST CATASTROPHE
BEING IN THE KNOW
CAPITALIZING ON SOCIAL CAPITAL AMID THE DEVALUATION OF INHERENT WORTH
FORGETTING TO REMEMBER THE PAST
INFORMATIONAL RELATIONSHIPS
TALKING AT, NOT SPEAKING WITH
DEFENDING ONE'S BODY BUT STILL HATING IT
ANXIETY
RANTING
ONESELF
EVADING SURVEILLANCE
BEING GREEN
HEIGHTENED ATOMIZATION
TRYING TO KEEP IN MIND THAT THE WORLD IS CRAZY, NOT US
UPGRADING
FEELING UNANCHORED IN A WIRELESS WORLD
STRUGGLING TO BE SEEN, HEARD, LOVED
AGAINST END-TIMES
REMAINING INVISIBLE
WORKING OUT
SCHOOLING ONESELF FOR JOBS THAT NO LONGER EXIST
AVOIDING EYE CONTACT BUT GAZING INTIMATELY INTO ONE'S SMART PHONE
HANGING ON TO A HOME, DESPITE LANDLORDS & BANKS
SATISFYING DESIRES NOT OF OUR OWN MAKING
STAYING HEALTHY WITHOUT HEALTH CARE
ALLEVIATING BOREDOM
HOPELESSNESS

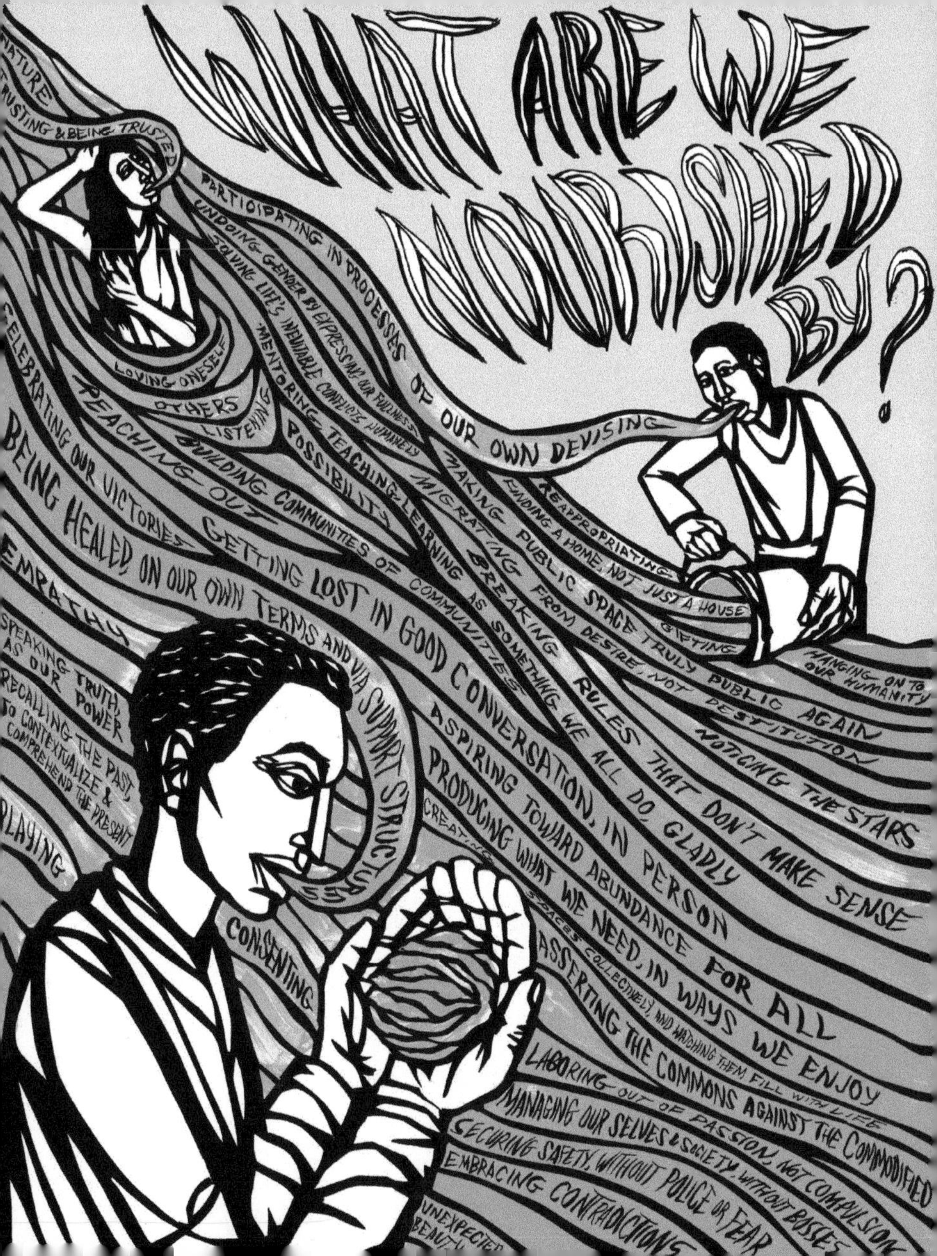

WHAT ARE WE NOURISHED BY?
NATURE
TRUSTING & BEING TRUSTED
PARTICIPATING IN PROCESSES OF OUR OWN DEVISING
UNDOING GENDER BY EXPRESSING OUR FULLNESS
SOLVING LIFE'S INEVITABLE CONFLICTS HUMANELY
LOVING ONESELF
OTHERS
LISTENING
MENTORING, TEACHING, LEARNING
AS SOMETHING WE ALL DO GLADLY
CELEBRATING OUR VICTORIES
REACHING OUT
BUILDING COMMUNITIES OF COMMUNITIES
POSSIBILITY
MAKING PUBLIC SPACE TRULY PUBLIC AGAIN
MIGRATING FROM DESIRE, NOT DESTITUTION
REAPPROPRIATING
FINDING A HOME, NOT JUST A HOUSE
GIFTING
HANGING ON TO OUR HUMANITY
BREAKING RULES THAT DON'T MAKE SENSE
NOTICING THE STARS
BEING HEALED ON OUR OWN TERMS AND VIA SUPPORT STRUCTURES
GETTING LOST IN GOOD CONVERSATION, IN PERSON
EMPATHY
SPEAKING TRUTH AS OUR POWER
RECALLING THE PAST, TO CONTEXTUALIZE & COMPREHEND THE PRESENT
PLAYING
ASPIRING TOWARD ABUNDANCE FOR ALL
PRODUCING WHAT WE NEED, IN WAYS WE ENJOY
CREATING SPACES COLLECTIVELY, AND WATCHING THEM FILL WITH LIFE
CONSENTING
ASSERTING THE COMMONS AGAINST THE COMMODIFIED
LABORING OUT OF PASSION, NOT COMPULSION
MANAGING OUR SELVES & SOCIETY, WITHOUT BOSSES
SECURING SAFETY, WITHOUT POLICE OR FEAR
EMBRACING CONTRADICTIONS
UNEXPECTED

WHAT TO KEEP

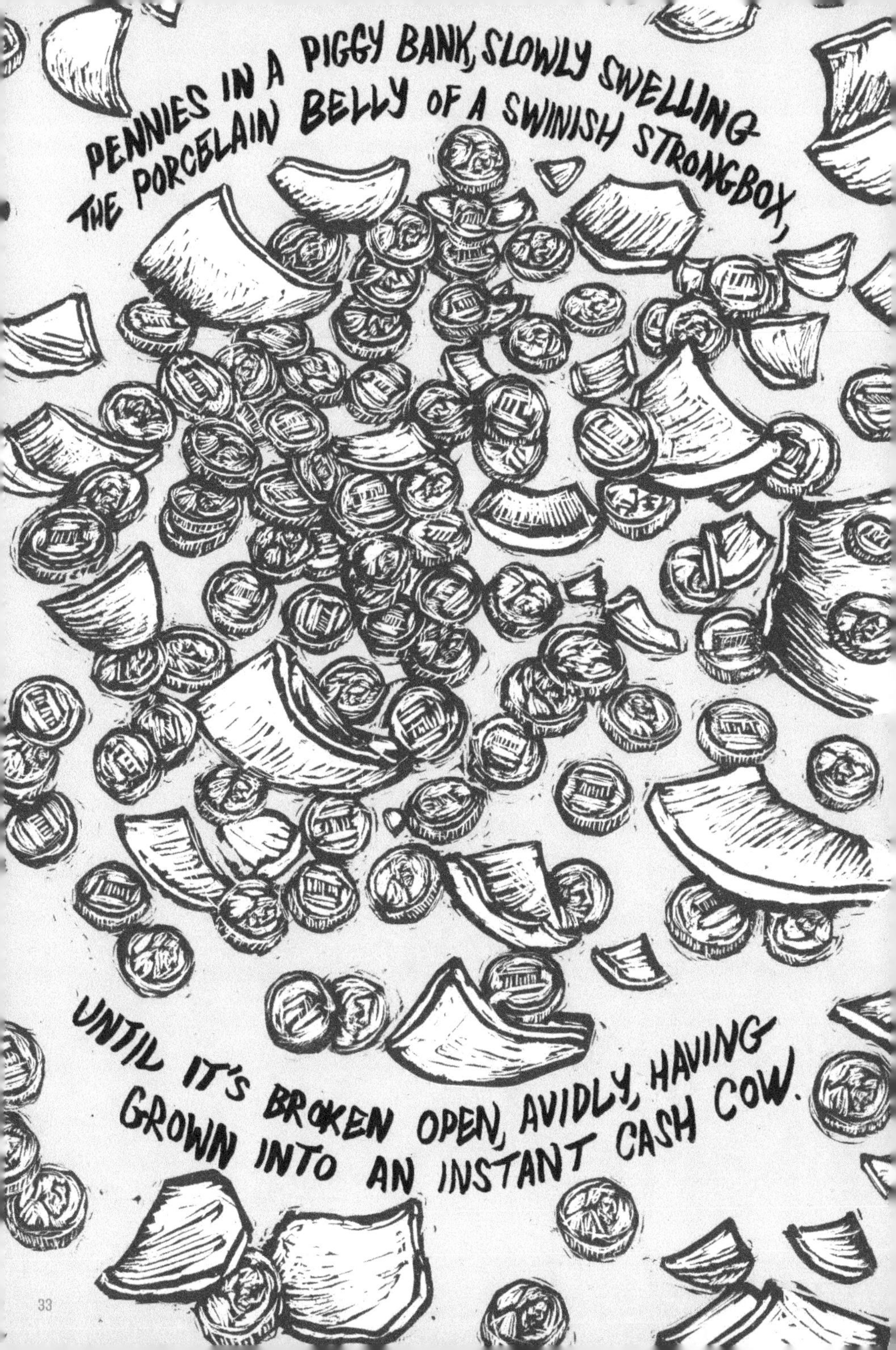
PENNIES IN A PIGGY BANK, SLOWLY SWELLING THE PORCELAIN BELLY OF A SWINISH STRONGBOX,
UNTIL IT'S BROKEN OPEN, AVIDLY, HAVING GROWN INTO AN INSTANT CASH COW.

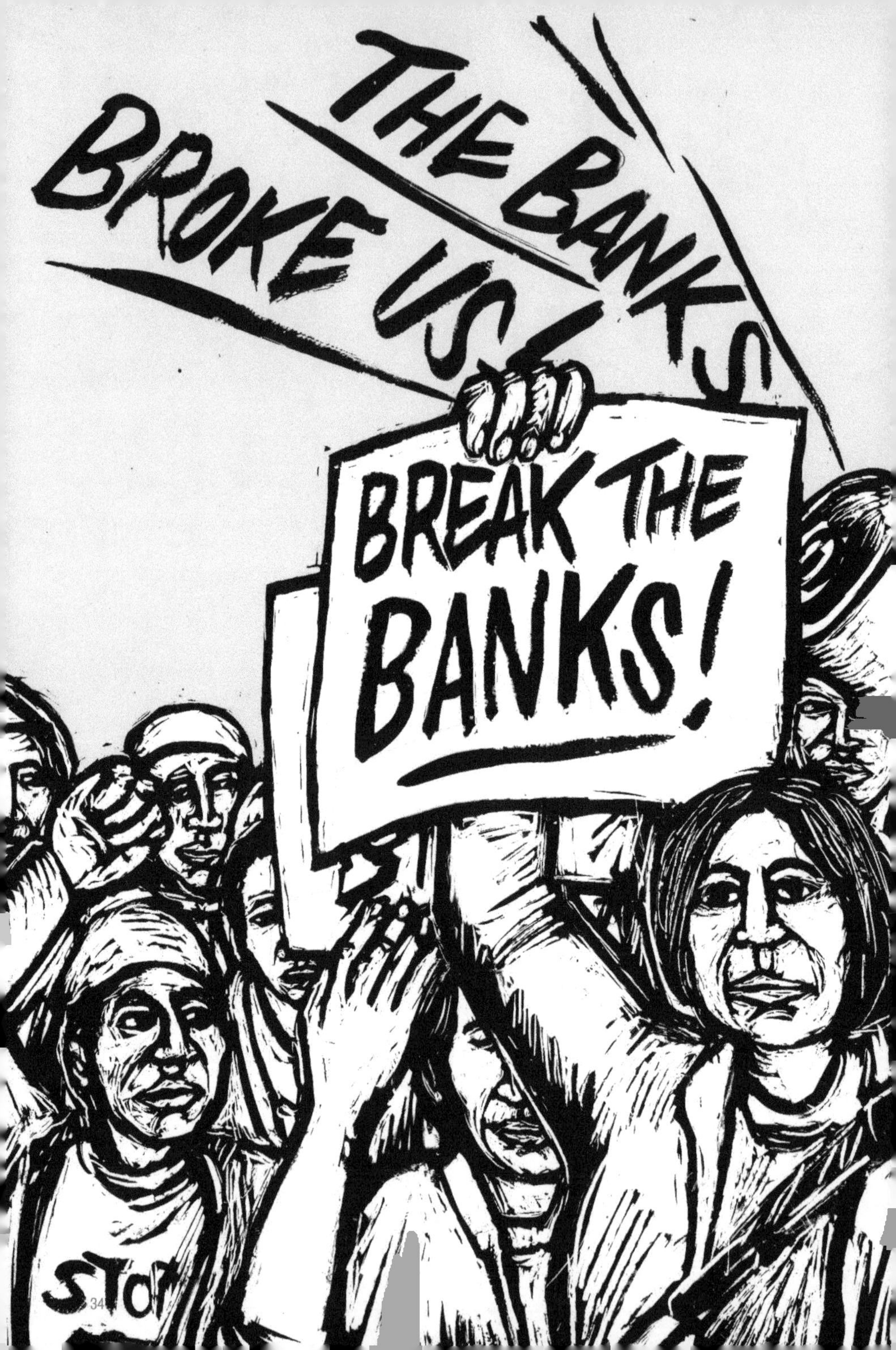
THE BANKS BROKE US
BREAK THE BANKS!
STOP

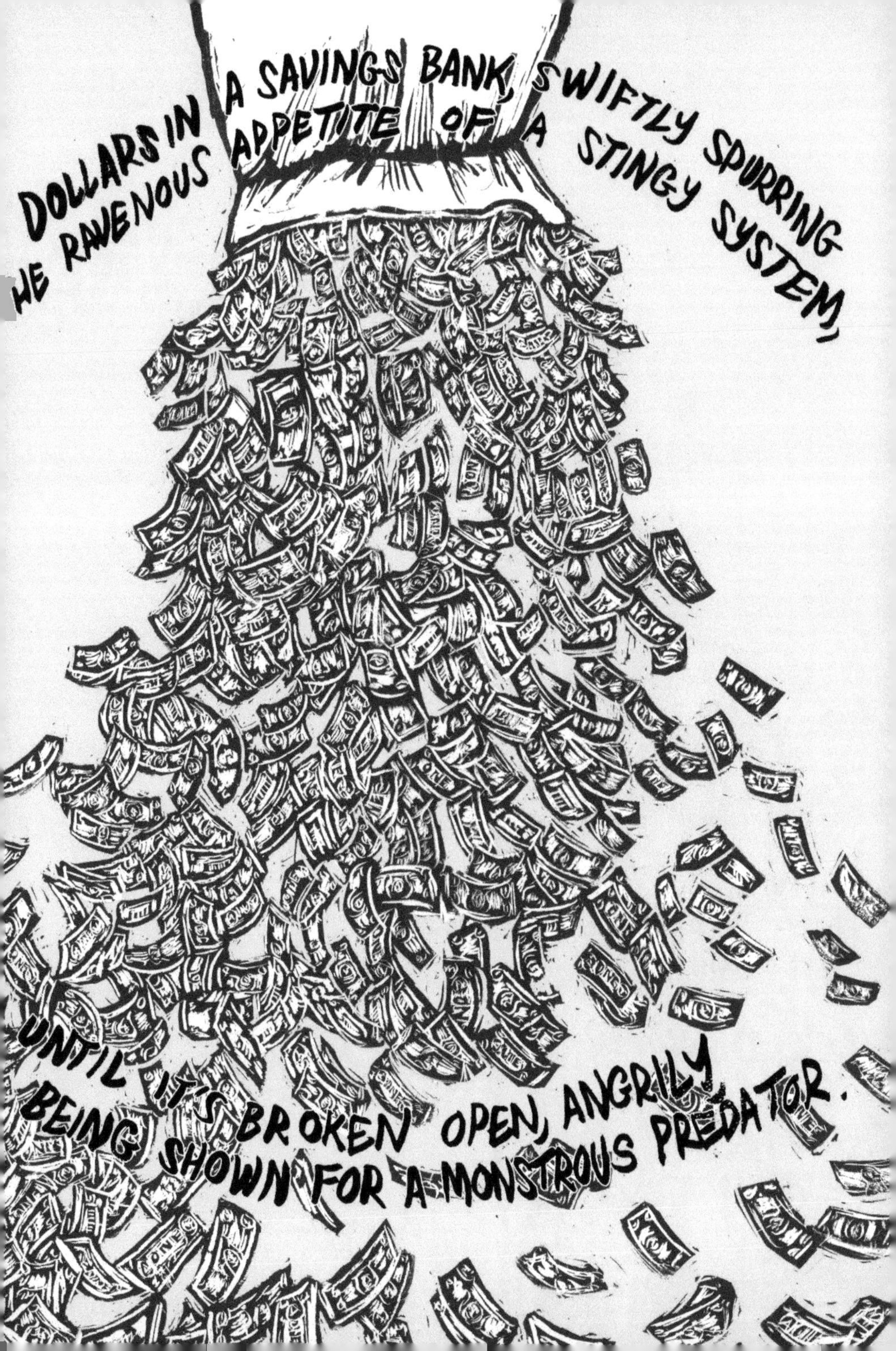
DOLLARS IN A SAVINGS BANK, SWIFTLY SPURRING
HE RAVENOUS APPETITE OF A STINGY SYSTEM,
UNTIL IT'S BROKEN OPEN, ANGRILY
BEING SHOWN FOR A MONSTROUS PREDATOR.

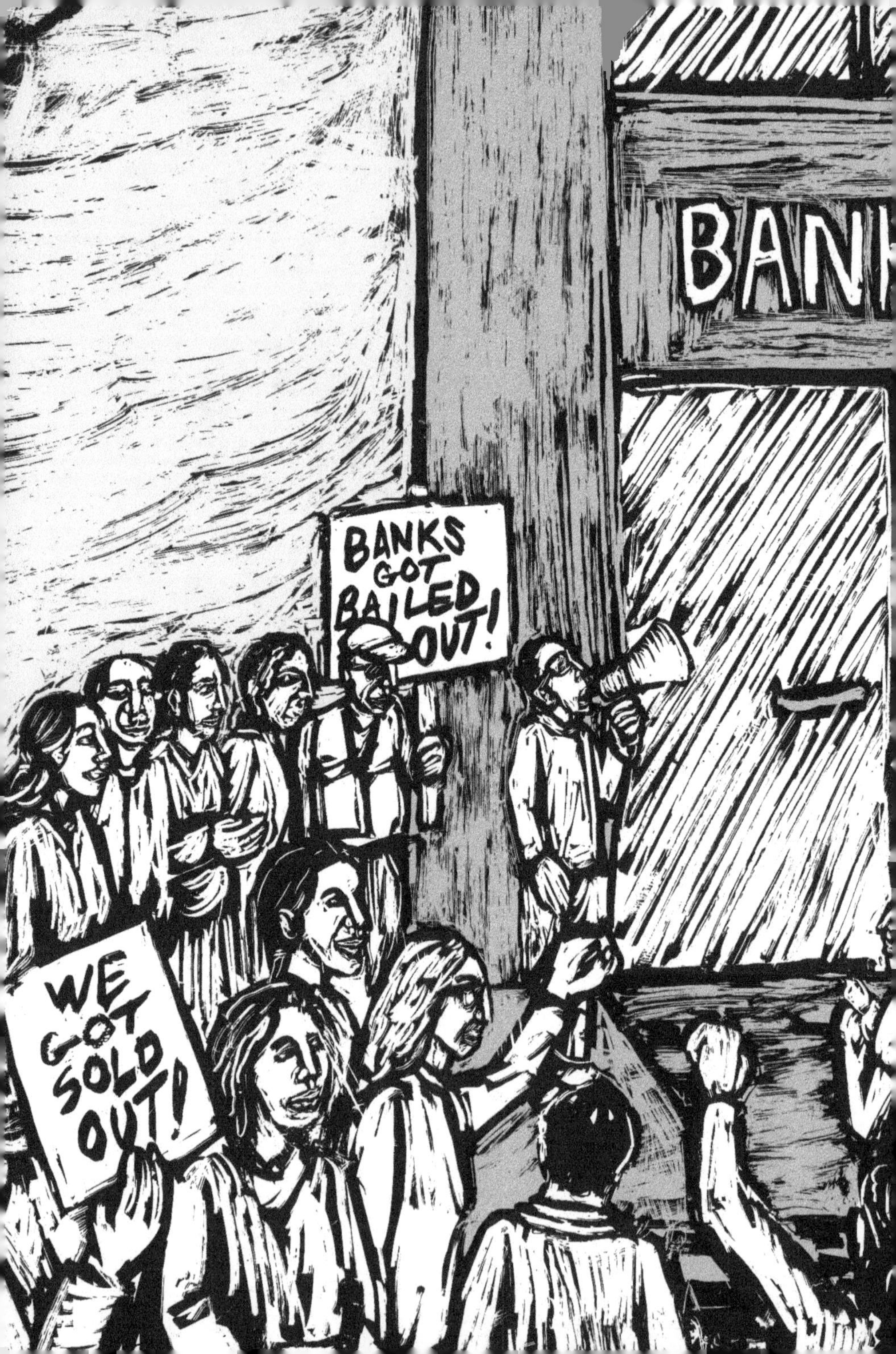
BANK
BANKS GOT BAILED OUT!
WE GOT SOLD OUT!

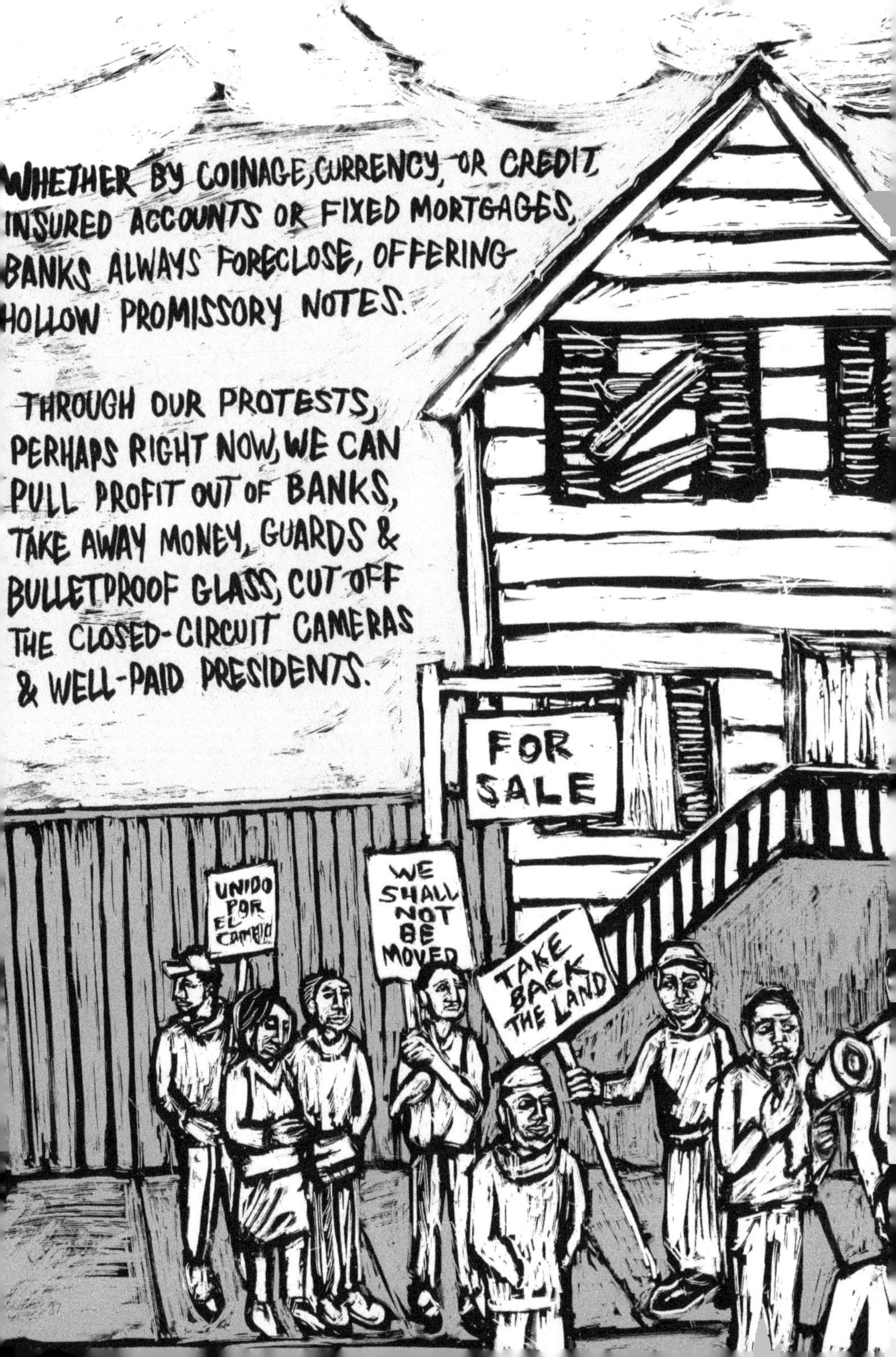
WHETHER BY COINAGE, CURRENCY, OR CREDIT, INSURED ACCOUNTS OR FIXED MORTGAGES, BANKS ALWAYS FORECLOSE, OFFERING HOLLOW PROMISSORY NOTES.
THROUGH OUR PROTESTS, PERHAPS RIGHT NOW, WE CAN PULL PROFIT OUT OF BANKS, TAKE AWAY MONEY, GUARDS & BULLETPROOF GLASS, CUT OFF THE CLOSED-CIRCUIT CAMERAS & WELL-PAID PRESIDENTS.
FOR SALE
UNIDO POR EL CAMBIO
WE SHALL NOT BE MOVED
TAKE BACK THE LAND

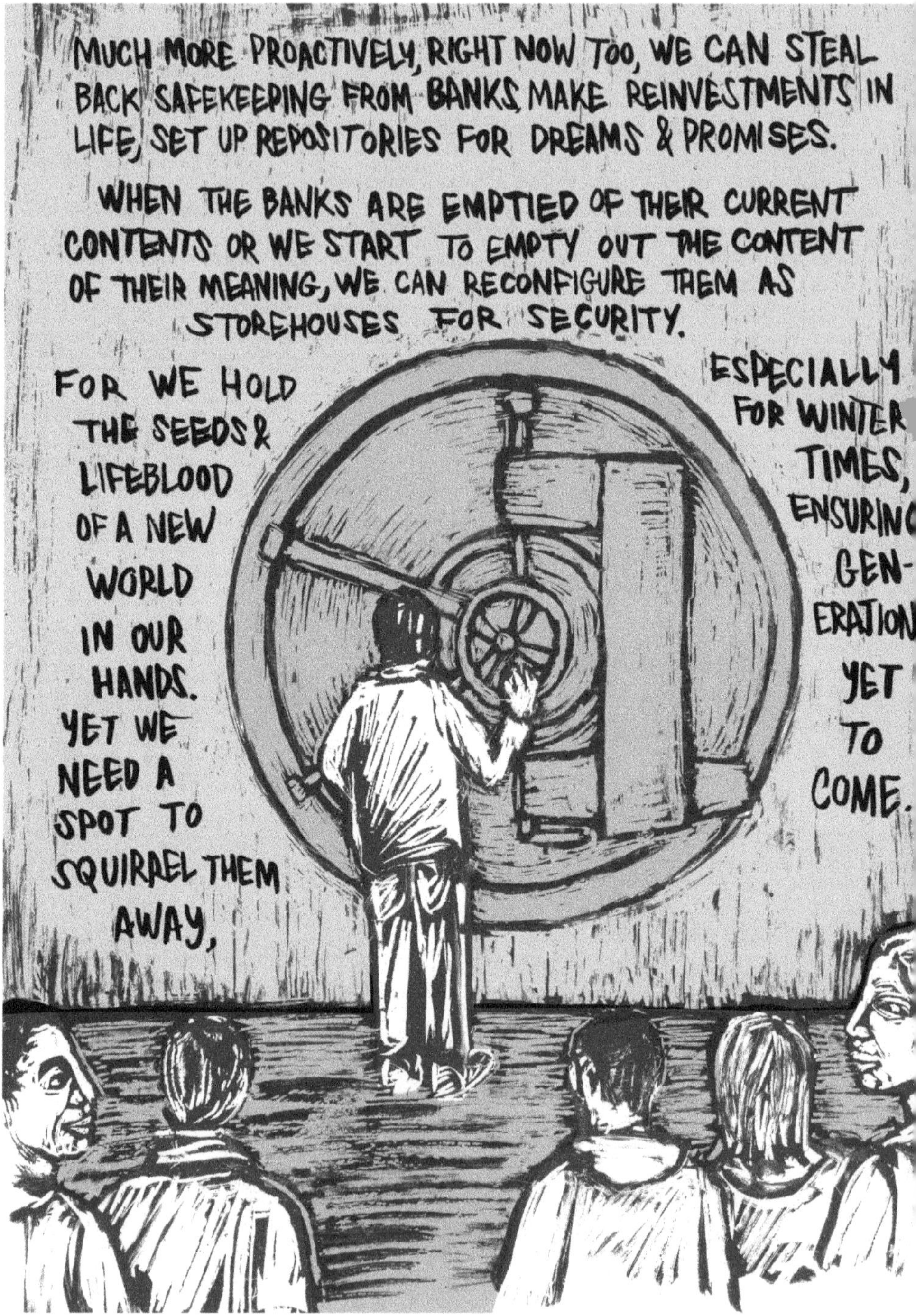
MUCH MORE PROACTIVELY, RIGHT NOW TOO, WE CAN STEAL BACK SAFEKEEPING FROM BANKS, MAKE REINVESTMENTS IN LIFE, SET UP REPOSITORIES FOR DREAMS & PROMISES.
WHEN THE BANKS ARE EMPTIED OF THEIR CURRENT CONTENTS OR WE START TO EMPTY OUT THE CONTENT OF THEIR MEANING, WE CAN RECONFIGURE THEM AS STOREHOUSES FOR SECURITY.
FOR WE HOLD THE SEEDS & LIFEBLOOD OF A NEW WORLD IN OUR HANDS. YET WE NEED A SPOT TO SQUIRREL THEM AWAY,
ESPECIALLY FOR WINTER TIMES, ENSURING GEN-ERATIONS YET TO COME.

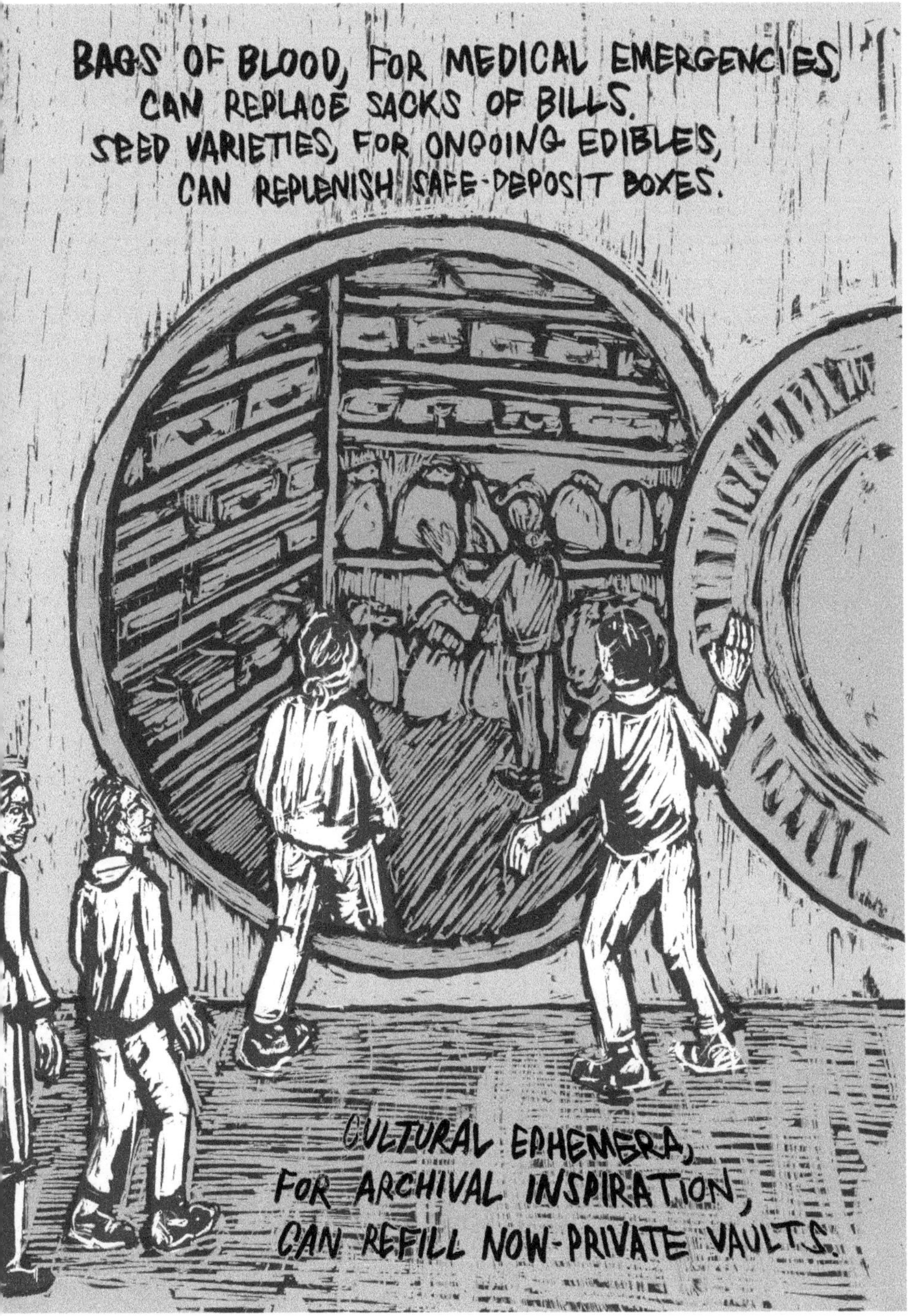
BAGS OF BLOOD, FOR MEDICAL EMERGENCIES,
CAN REPLACE SACKS OF BILLS.
SEED VARIETIES, FOR ONGOING EDIBLES,
CAN REPLENISH SAFE-DEPOSIT BOXES.
CULTURAL EPHEMERA,
FOR ARCHIVAL INSPIRATION,
CAN REFILL NOW-PRIVATE VAULTS.

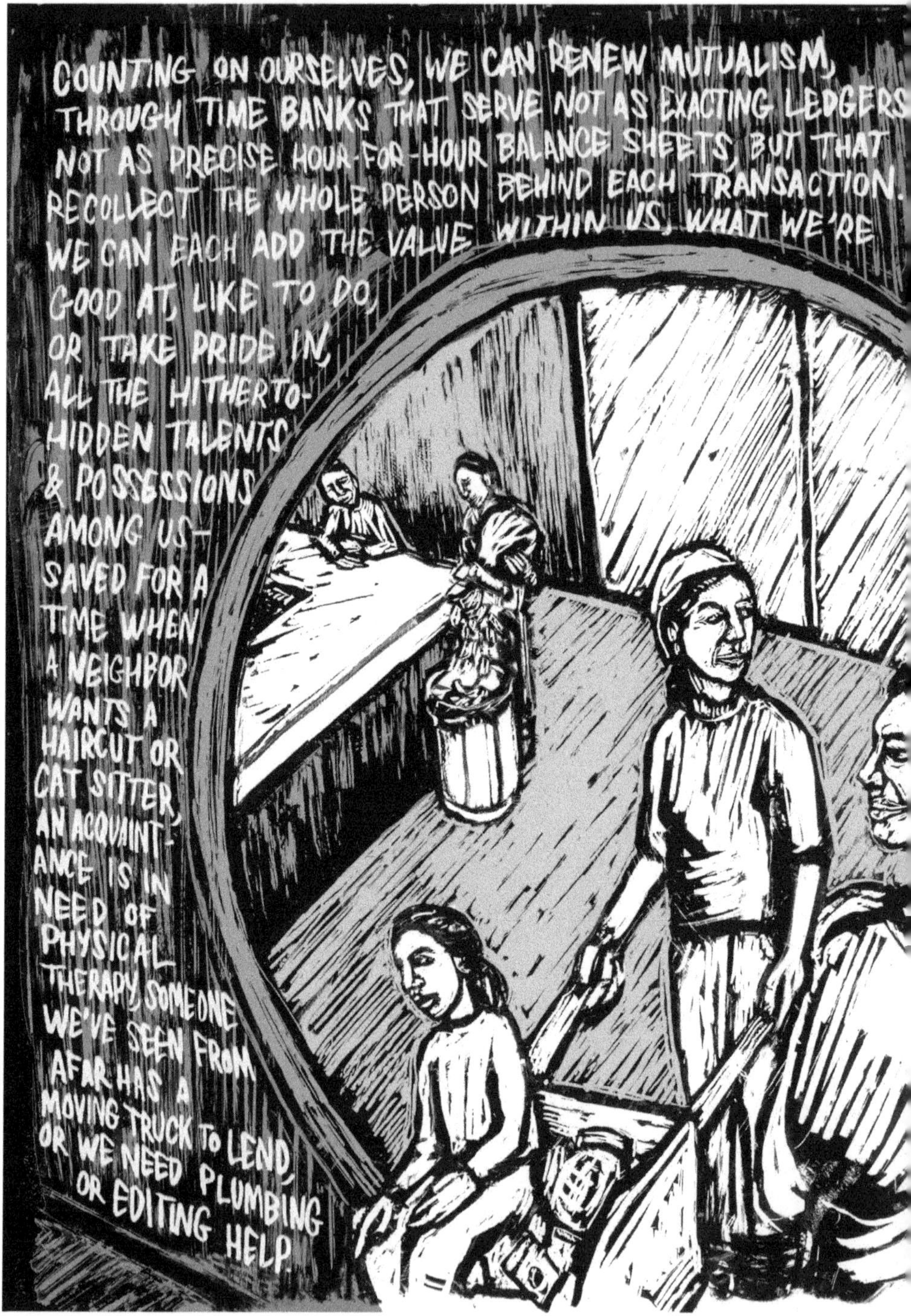
COUNTING ON OURSELVES, WE CAN RENEW MUTUALISM, THROUGH TIME BANKS THAT SERVE NOT AS EXACTING LEDGERS, NOT AS PRECISE HOUR-FOR-HOUR BALANCE SHEETS, BUT THAT RECOLLECT THE WHOLE PERSON BEHIND EACH TRANSACTION. WE CAN EACH ADD THE VALUE WITHIN US, WHAT WE'RE GOOD AT, LIKE TO DO, OR TAKE PRIDE IN, ALL THE HITHERTO-HIDDEN TALENTS & POSSESSIONS AMONG US—SAVED FOR A TIME WHEN A NEIGHBOR WANTS A HAIRCUT OR CAT SITTER, AN ACQUAINTANCE IS IN NEED OF PHYSICAL THERAPY, SOMEONE WE'VE SEEN FROM AFAR HAS A MOVING TRUCK TO LEND, OR WE NEED PLUMBING OR EDITING HELP.

LOWLY BUT SURELY,
HE BANK AS CAPITALIST
DIFICE WILL BECOME
UNNECESSARY AS WE
ECOME INDEBTED, WITHOUT
IN OR GREED, TO THE
ORTH OF EACH OTHER.

EAS, FOOD, DATA, SKILLS,
ARTIFACTS, RESOURCES,
MEMORIES
& MORE—

BANK O

COMING
SOON
SEED
EXCHANGE

ALL CAN ACCRUE OUR SHARED & SHAREABLE
INTEREST, BY DISMANTLING THE BANK AS WE KNOW
IT & BANKING ON THE COMMONS INSTEAD.

BORROWING FROM THE LIBRARY

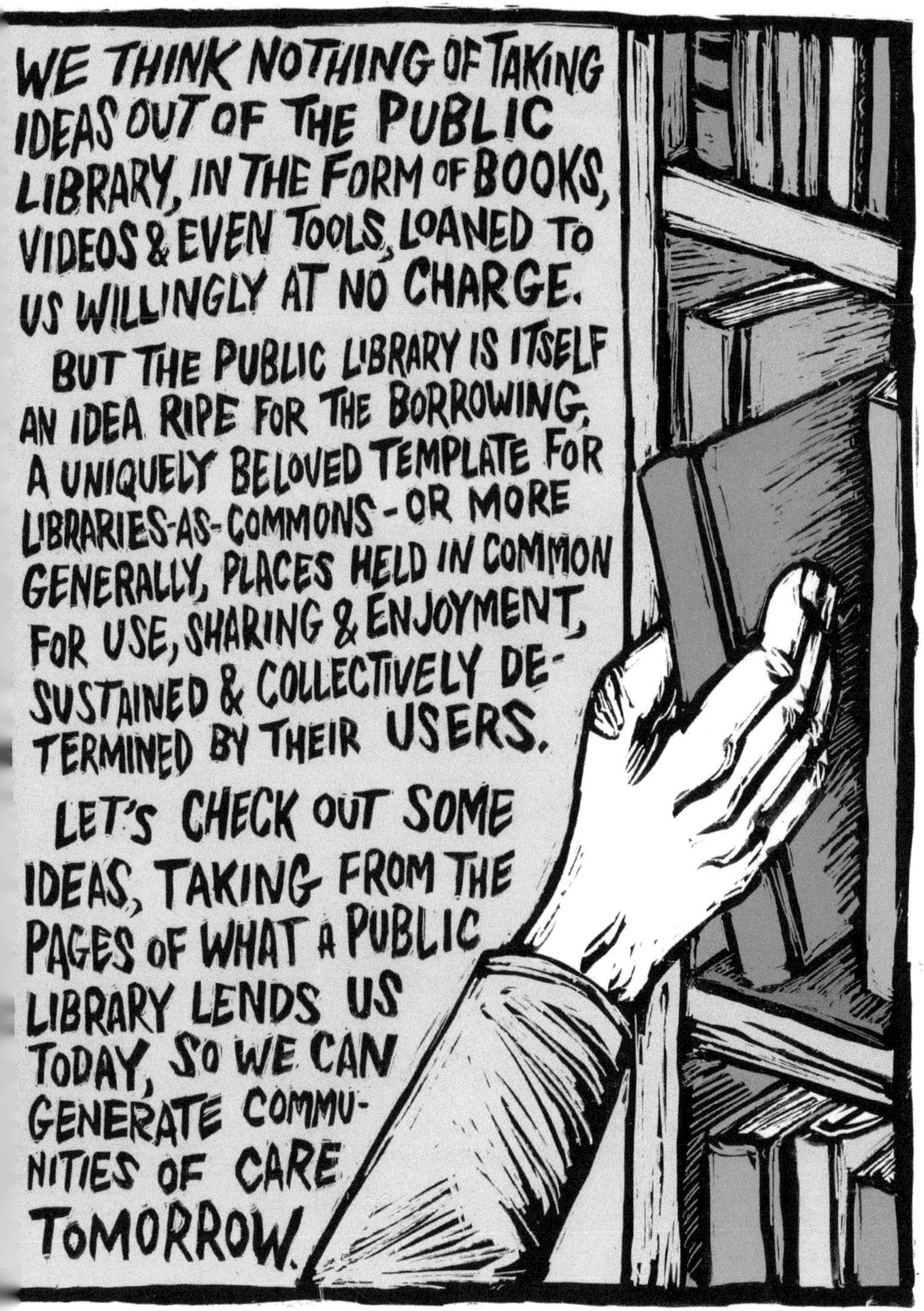
WE THINK NOTHING OF TAKING IDEAS OUT OF THE PUBLIC LIBRARY, IN THE FORM OF BOOKS, VIDEOS & EVEN TOOLS, LOANED TO US WILLINGLY AT NO CHARGE.
BUT THE PUBLIC LIBRARY IS ITSELF AN IDEA RIPE FOR THE BORROWING, A UNIQUELY BELOVED TEMPLATE FOR LIBRARIES-AS-COMMONS - OR MORE GENERALLY, PLACES HELD IN COMMON FOR USE, SHARING & ENJOYMENT, SUSTAINED & COLLECTIVELY DETERMINED BY THEIR USERS.
LET'S CHECK OUT SOME IDEAS, TAKING FROM THE PAGES OF WHAT A PUBLIC LIBRARY LENDS US TODAY, SO WE CAN GENERATE COMMUNITIES OF CARE TOMORROW.

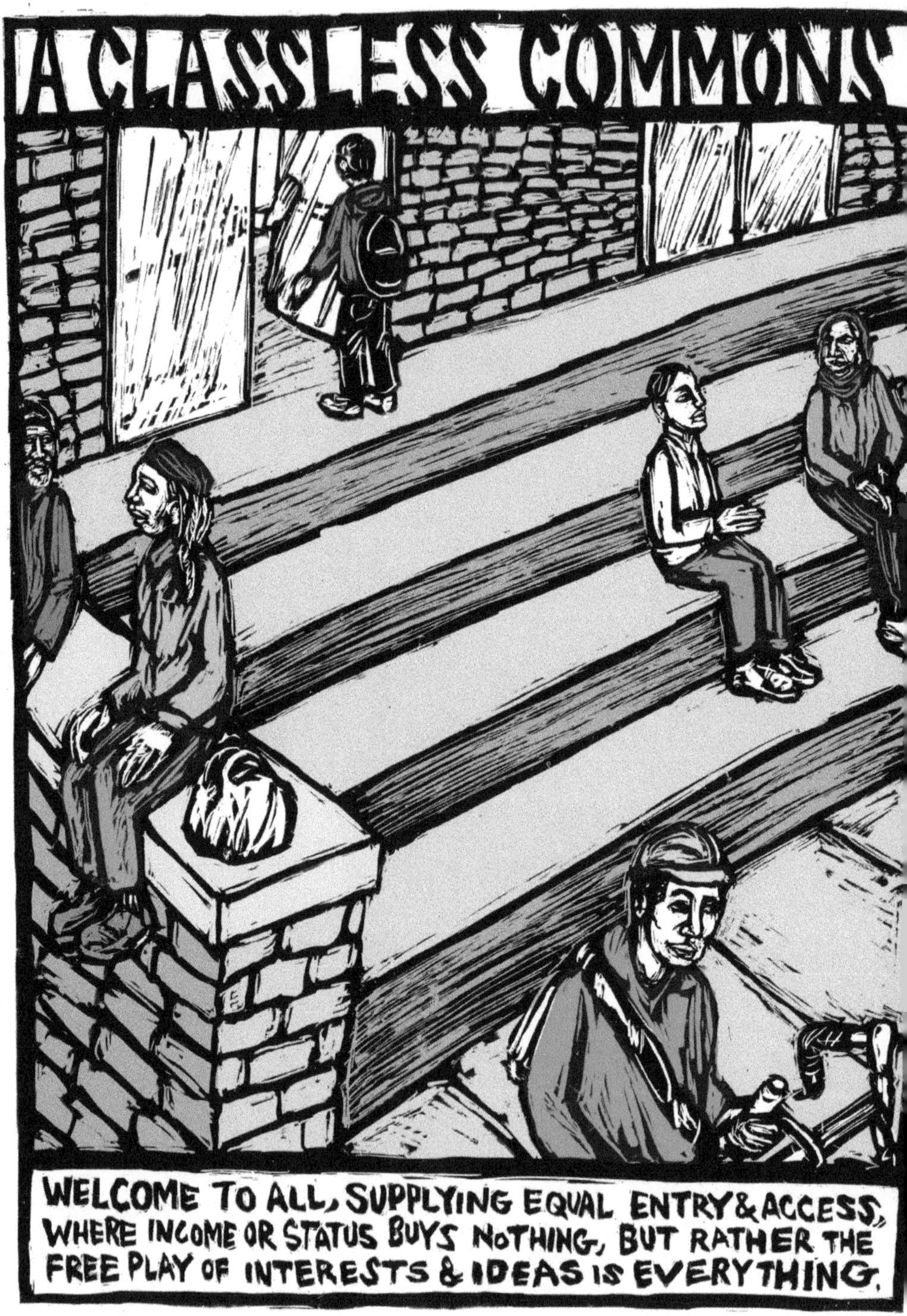
A CLASSLESS COMMONS
WELCOME TO ALL, SUPPLYING EQUAL ENTRY & ACCESS, WHERE INCOME OR STATUS BUYS NOTHING, BUT RATHER THE FREE PLAY OF INTERESTS & IDEAS IS EVERYTHING.

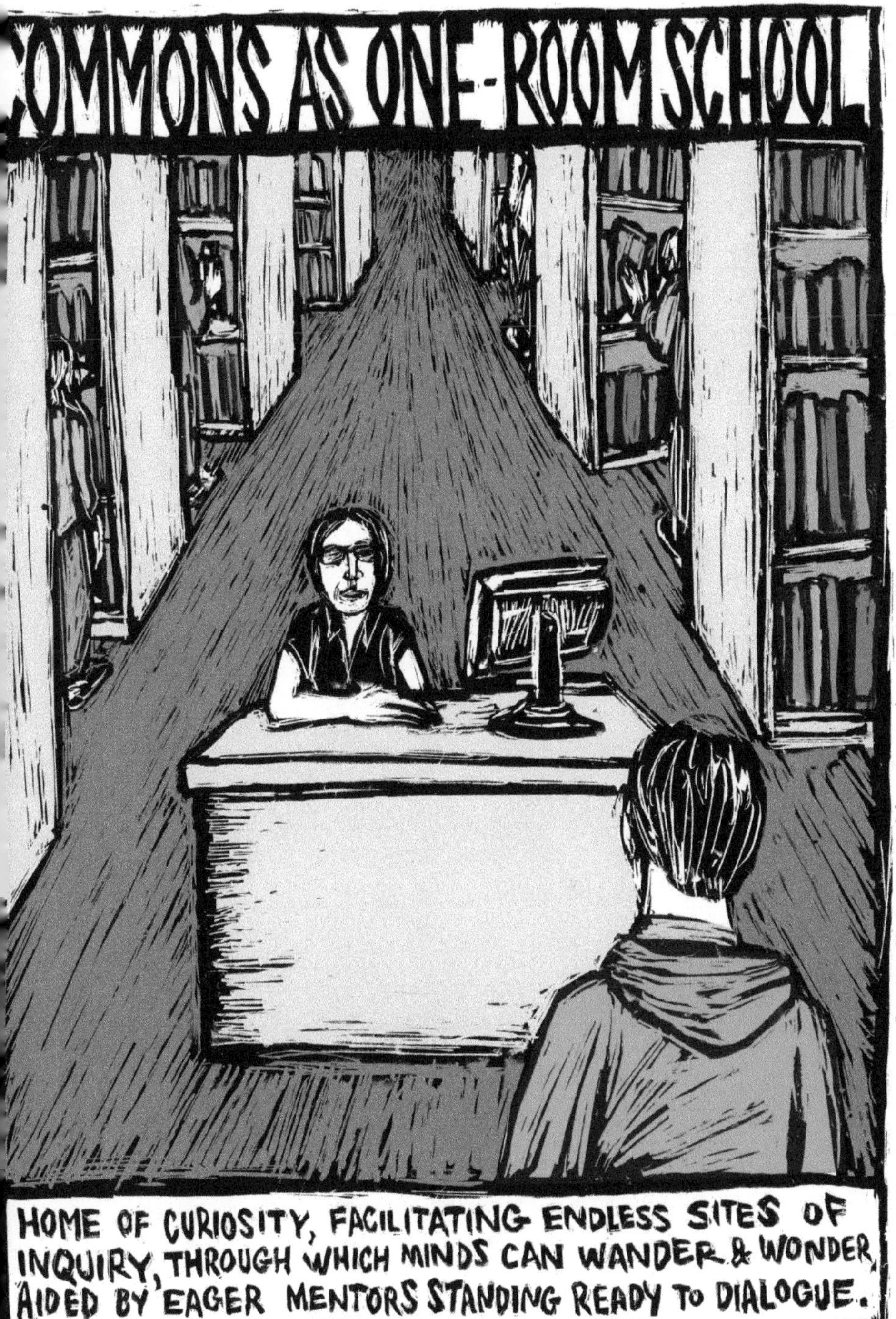
COMMONS AS ONE-ROOM SCHOOL
HOME OF CURIOSITY, FACILITATING ENDLESS SITES OF INQUIRY, THROUGH WHICH MINDS CAN WANDER & WONDER, AIDED BY EAGER MENTORS STANDING READY TO DIALOGUE.

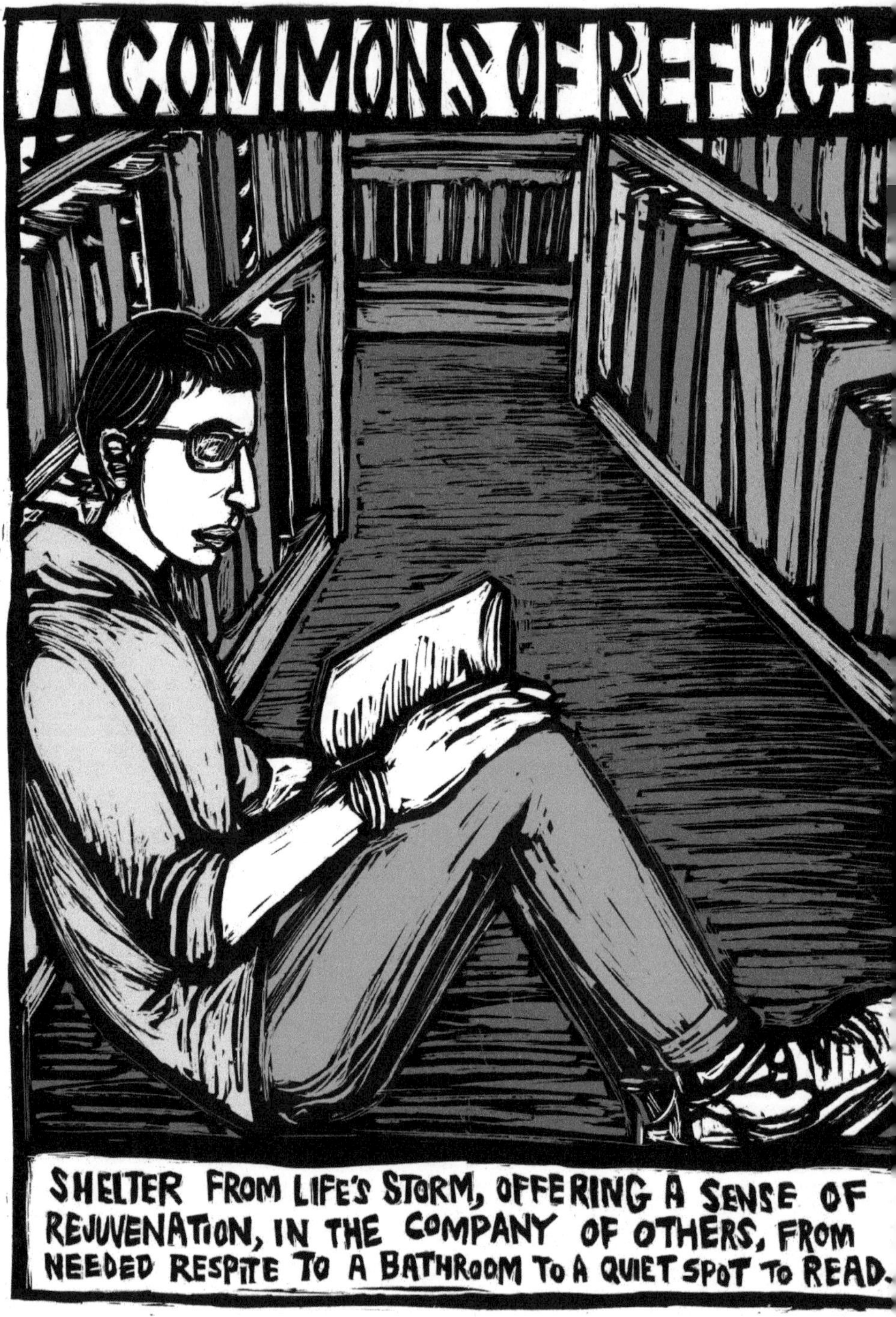
A COMMONS OF REFUGE
SHELTER FROM LIFE'S STORM, OFFERING A SENSE OF REJUVENATION, IN THE COMPANY OF OTHERS, FROM NEEDED RESPITE TO A BATHROOM TO A QUIET SPOT TO READ.

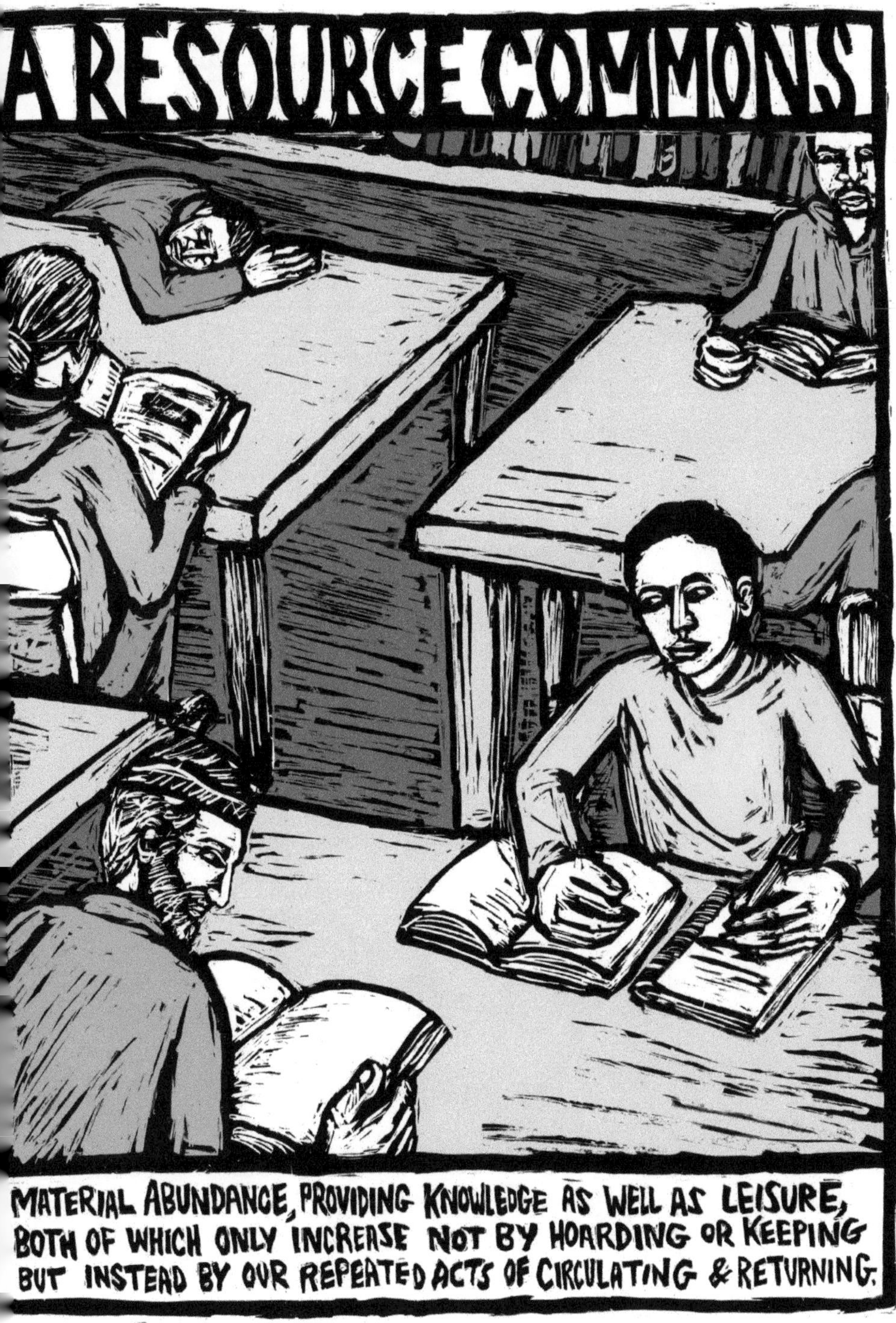
A RESOURCE COMMONS
MATERIAL ABUNDANCE, PROVIDING KNOWLEDGE AS WELL AS LEISURE, BOTH OF WHICH ONLY INCREASE NOT BY HOARDING OR KEEPING BUT INSTEAD BY OUR REPEATED ACTS OF CIRCULATING & RETURNING.

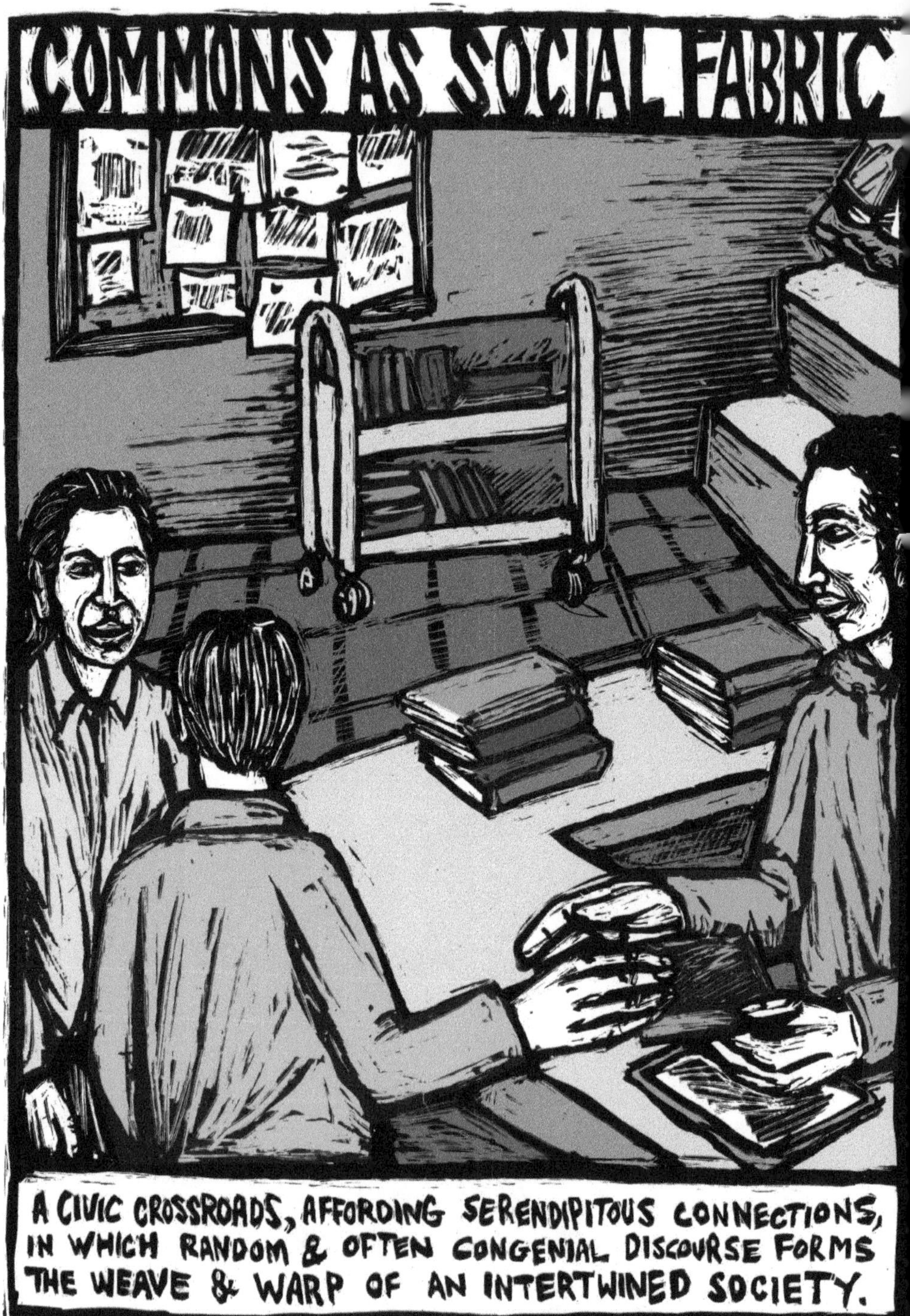
COMMONS AS SOCIAL FABRIC
A CIVIC CROSSROADS, AFFORDING SERENDIPITOUS CONNECTIONS, IN WHICH RANDOM & OFTEN CONGENIAL DISCOURSE FORMS THE WEAVE & WARP OF AN INTERTWINED SOCIETY.

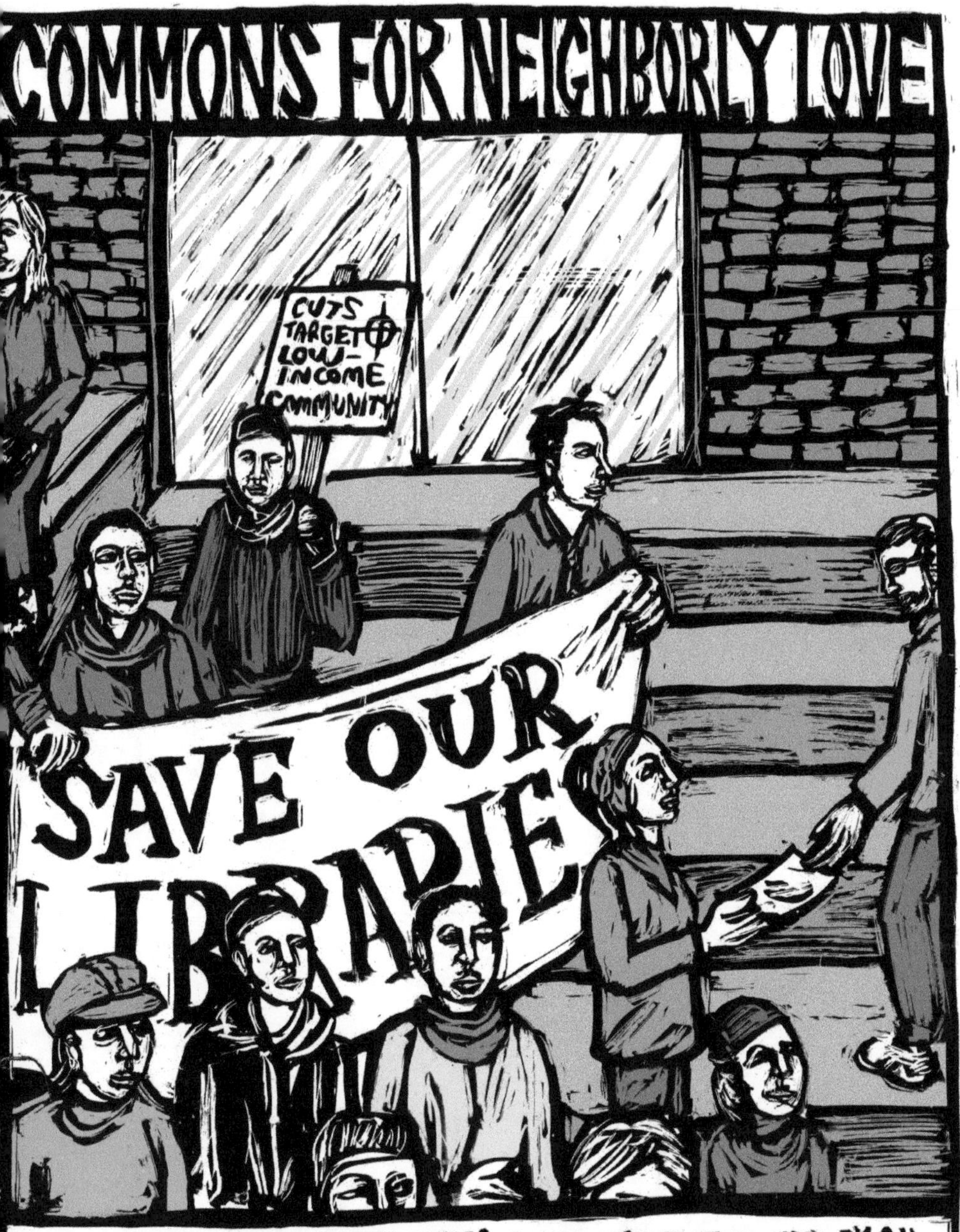
COMMONS FOR NEIGHBORLY LOVE
CUTS TARGET LOW-INCOME COMMUNITY
SAVE OUR
A COMMUNAL GOOD, EXEMPLIFYING A USE VALUE TREASURED BY ALL, AS A SOURCE OF SOCIAL RESISTANCE WHEN THREATENED BY CUTS, YET ALSO A WELLSPRING OF SOCIAL RECONSTRUCTION, TOWARD A FUTURE PERFECT.

WE SHOULD THINK EVERYTHING OF PUBLIC LIBRARIES - BORROWING IDEAS TO DEVELOP NEWFANGLED, AUTONOMOUS COMMONS, THE FRESH LEAVES IN OUR STORY OF HOW WE INTERDEPENDENTLY ANIMATE PROTECTION, EQUITY & SOCIABILITY, THINGS & THOUGHT, EMPATHY & WISDOM, NURTURING ALL SORTS OF GOODS & SPACES & FLIGHTS OF FANCY BEYOND BOOKS.

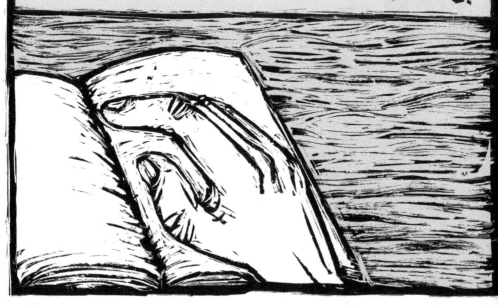

PICKING UP THE PARK

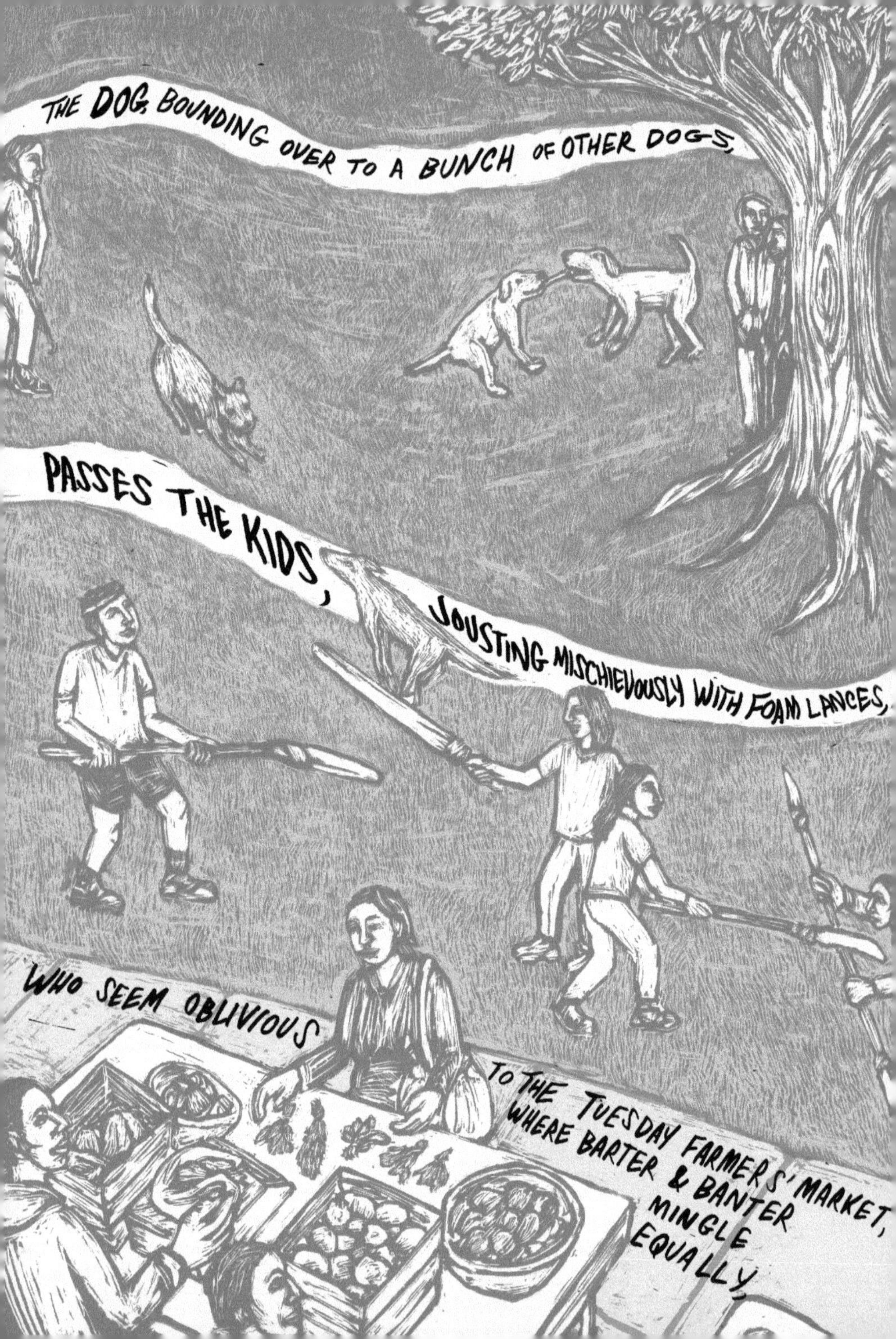
THE DOG, BOUNDING OVER TO A BUNCH OF OTHER DOGS,
PASSES THE KIDS,
JOUSTING MISCHIEVOUSLY WITH FOAM LANCES,
WHO SEEM OBLIVIOUS
TO THE TUESDAY FARMERS' MARKET, WHERE BARTER & BANTER MINGLE EQUALLY,

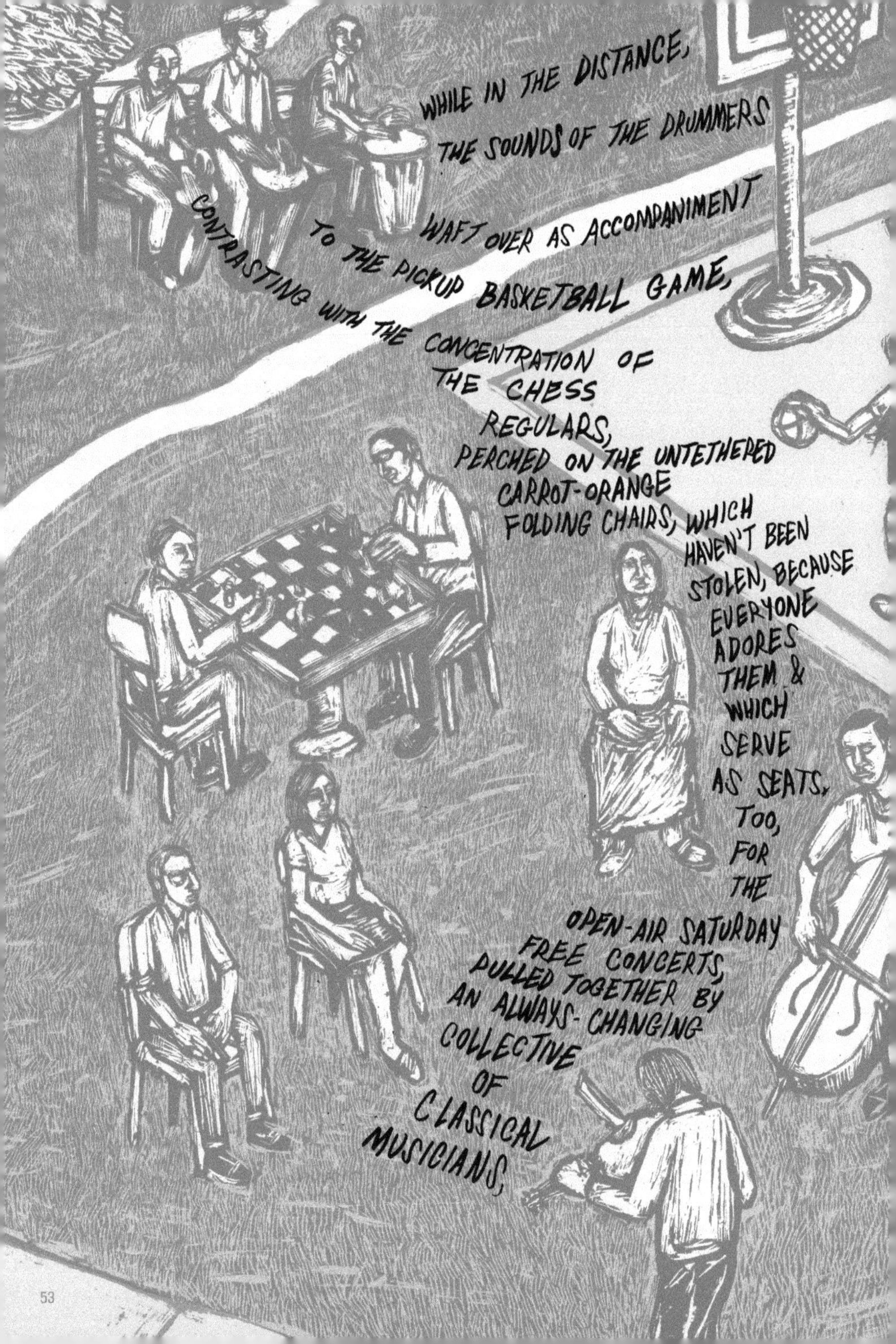

WHILE IN THE DISTANCE,
THE SOUNDS OF THE DRUMMERS
WAFT OVER AS ACCOMPANIMENT
TO THE PICKUP BASKETBALL GAME,
CONTRASTING WITH THE CONCENTRATION OF
THE CHESS
REGULARS,
PERCHED ON THE UNTETHERED
CARROT-ORANGE
FOLDING CHAIRS, WHICH
HAVEN'T BEEN
STOLEN, BECAUSE
EVERYONE
ADORES
THEM &
WHICH
SERVE
AS SEATS,
TOO,
FOR
THE
OPEN-AIR SATURDAY
FREE CONCERTS,
PULLED TOGETHER BY
AN ALWAYS-CHANGING
COLLECTIVE
OF
CLASSICAL
MUSICIANS,

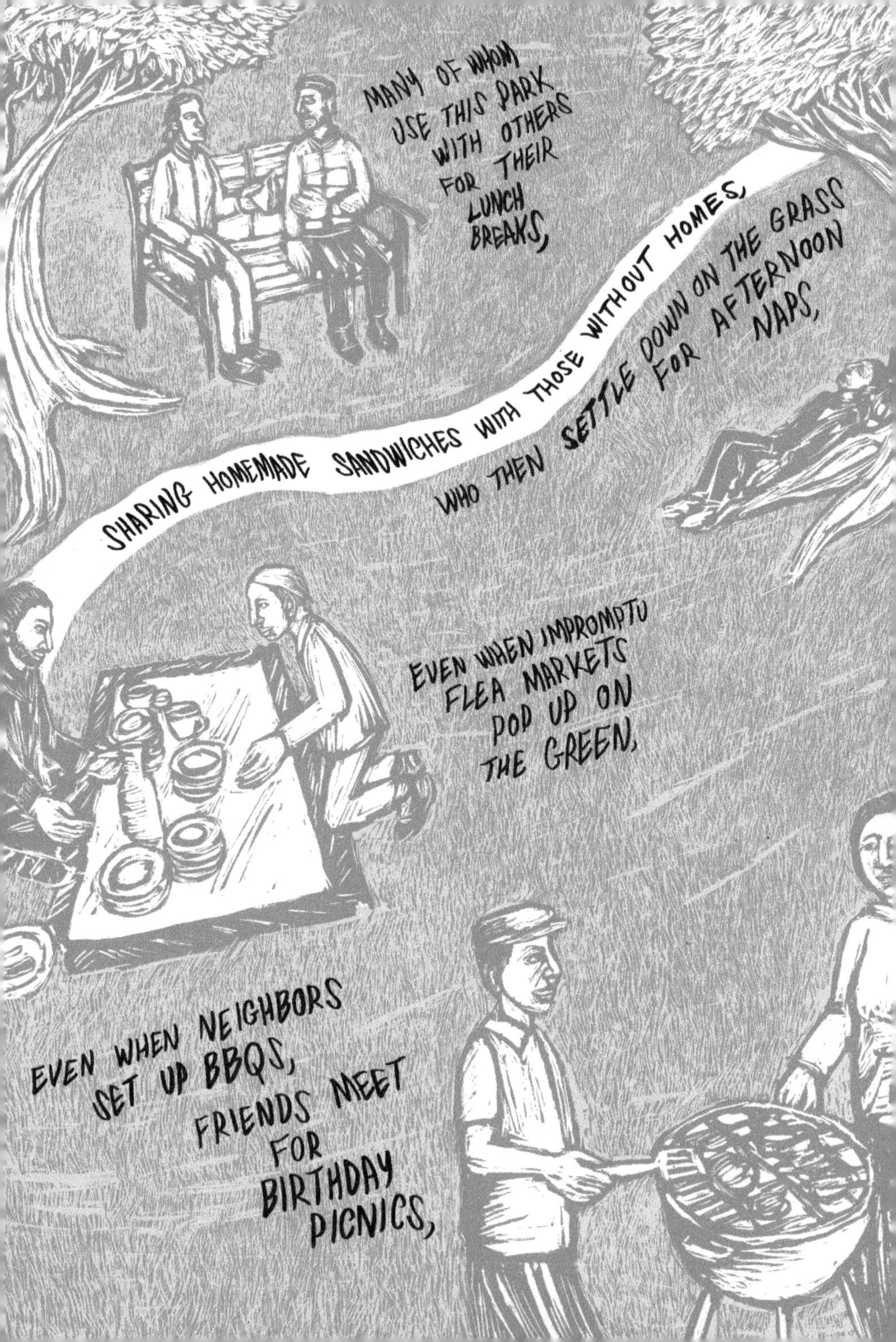
MANY OF WHOM USE THIS PARK WITH OTHERS FOR THEIR LUNCH BREAKS,
SHARING HOMEMADE SANDWICHES WITH THOSE WITHOUT HOMES,
WHO THEN SETTLE DOWN ON THE GRASS FOR AFTERNOON NAPS,
EVEN WHEN IMPROMPTU FLEA MARKETS POP UP ON THE GREEN,
EVEN WHEN NEIGHBORS SET UP BBQS,
FRIENDS MEET FOR BIRTHDAY PICNICS,

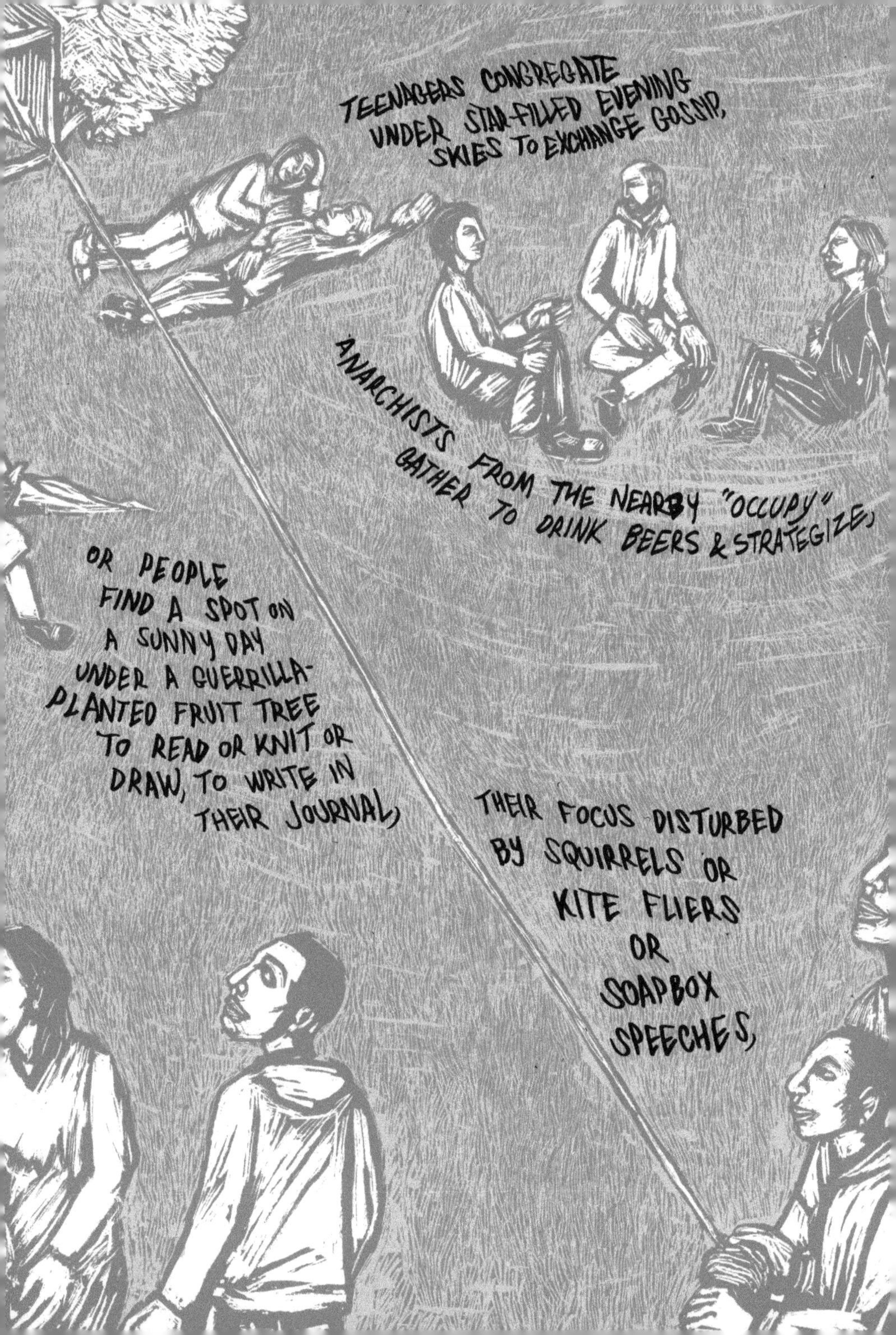
TEENAGERS CONGREGATE UNDER STAR-FILLED EVENING SKIES TO EXCHANGE GOSSIP,
ANARCHISTS FROM THE NEARBY "OCCUPY" GATHER TO DRINK BEERS & STRATEGIZE,
OR PEOPLE FIND A SPOT ON A SUNNY DAY UNDER A GUERRILLA-PLANTED FRUIT TREE TO READ OR KNIT OR DRAW, TO WRITE IN THEIR JOURNAL,
THEIR FOCUS DISTURBED BY SQUIRRELS OR KITE FLIERS OR SOAPBOX SPEECHES,

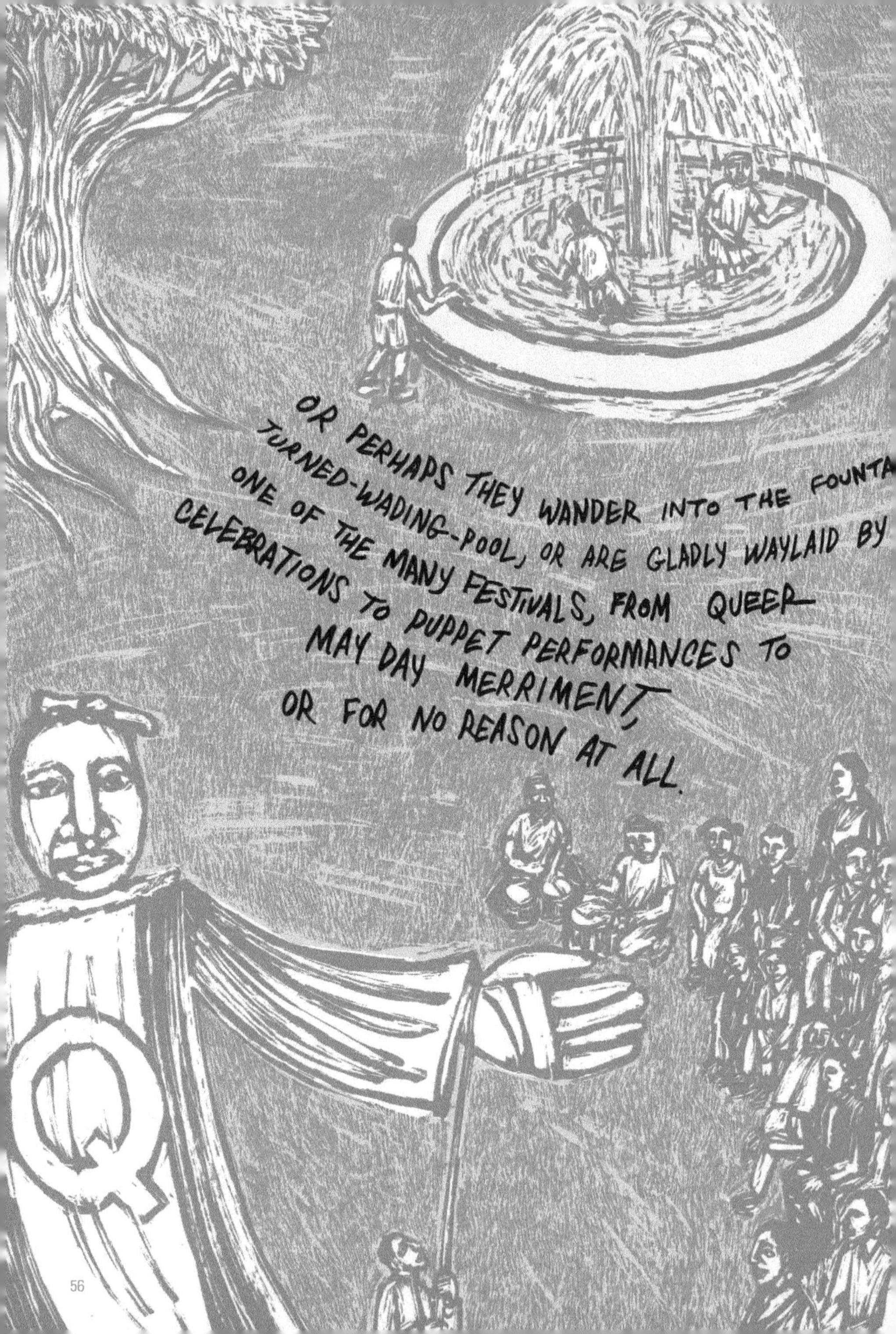
OR PERHAPS THEY WANDER INTO THE FOUNTA
TURNED-WADING-POOL, OR ARE GLADLY WAYLAID BY
ONE OF THE MANY FESTIVALS, FROM QUEER
CELEBRATIONS TO PUPPET PERFORMANCES TO
MAY DAY MERRIMENT,
OR FOR NO REASON AT ALL.

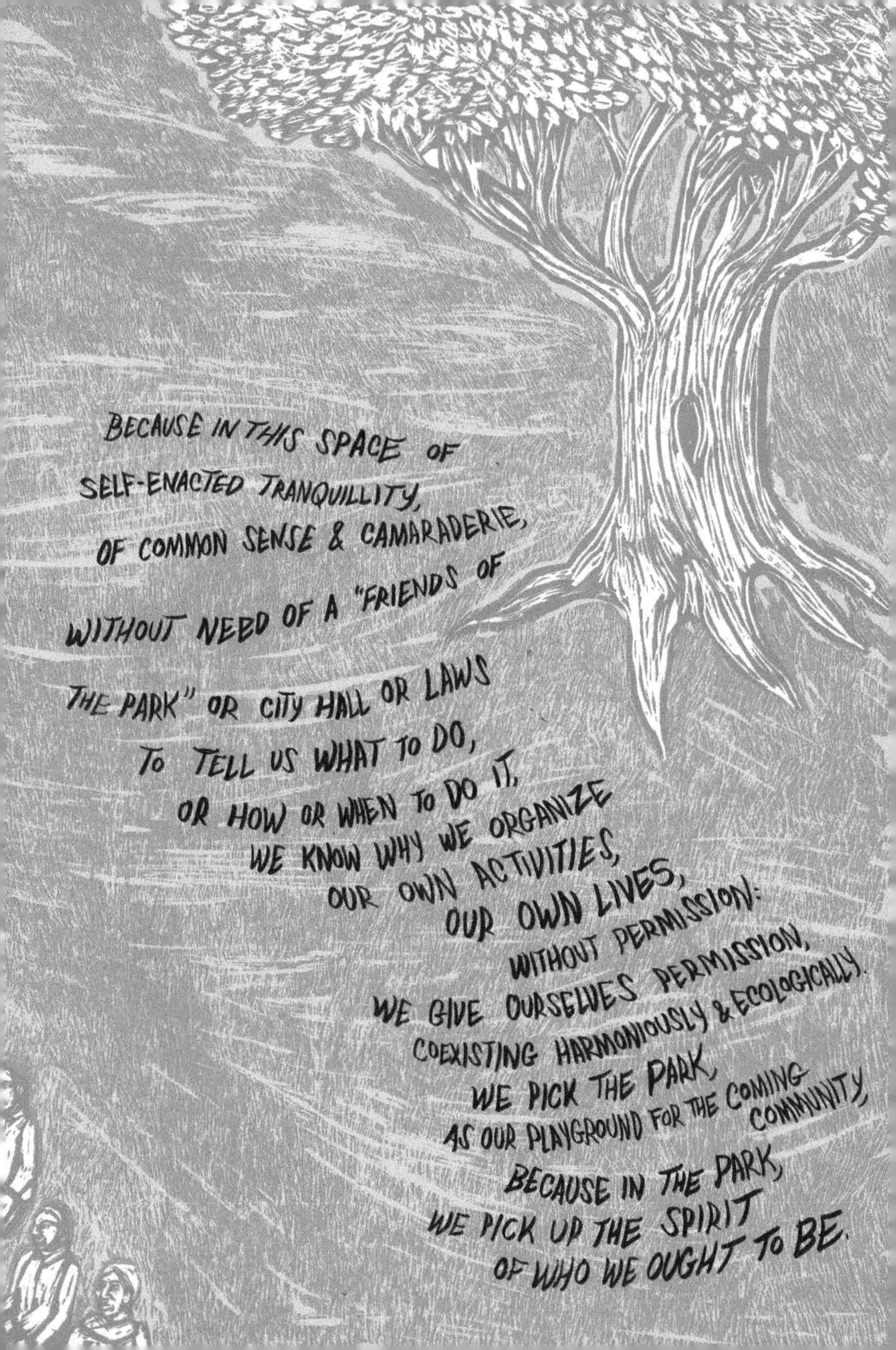
BECAUSE IN THIS SPACE OF
SELF-ENACTED TRANQUILLITY,
OF COMMON SENSE & CAMARADERIE,
WITHOUT NEED OF A "FRIENDS OF
THE PARK" OR CITY HALL OR LAWS
TO TELL US WHAT TO DO,
OR HOW OR WHEN TO DO IT,
WE KNOW WHY WE ORGANIZE
OUR OWN ACTIVITIES,
OUR OWN LIVES,
WITHOUT PERMISSION:
WE GIVE OURSELVES PERMISSION,
COEXISTING HARMONIOUSLY & ECOLOGICALLY.
WE PICK THE PARK,
AS OUR PLAYGROUND FOR THE COMING COMMUNITY,
BECAUSE IN THE PARK,
WE PICK UP THE SPIRIT
OF WHO WE OUGHT TO BE.

PATHS TOWARD UTOPIA

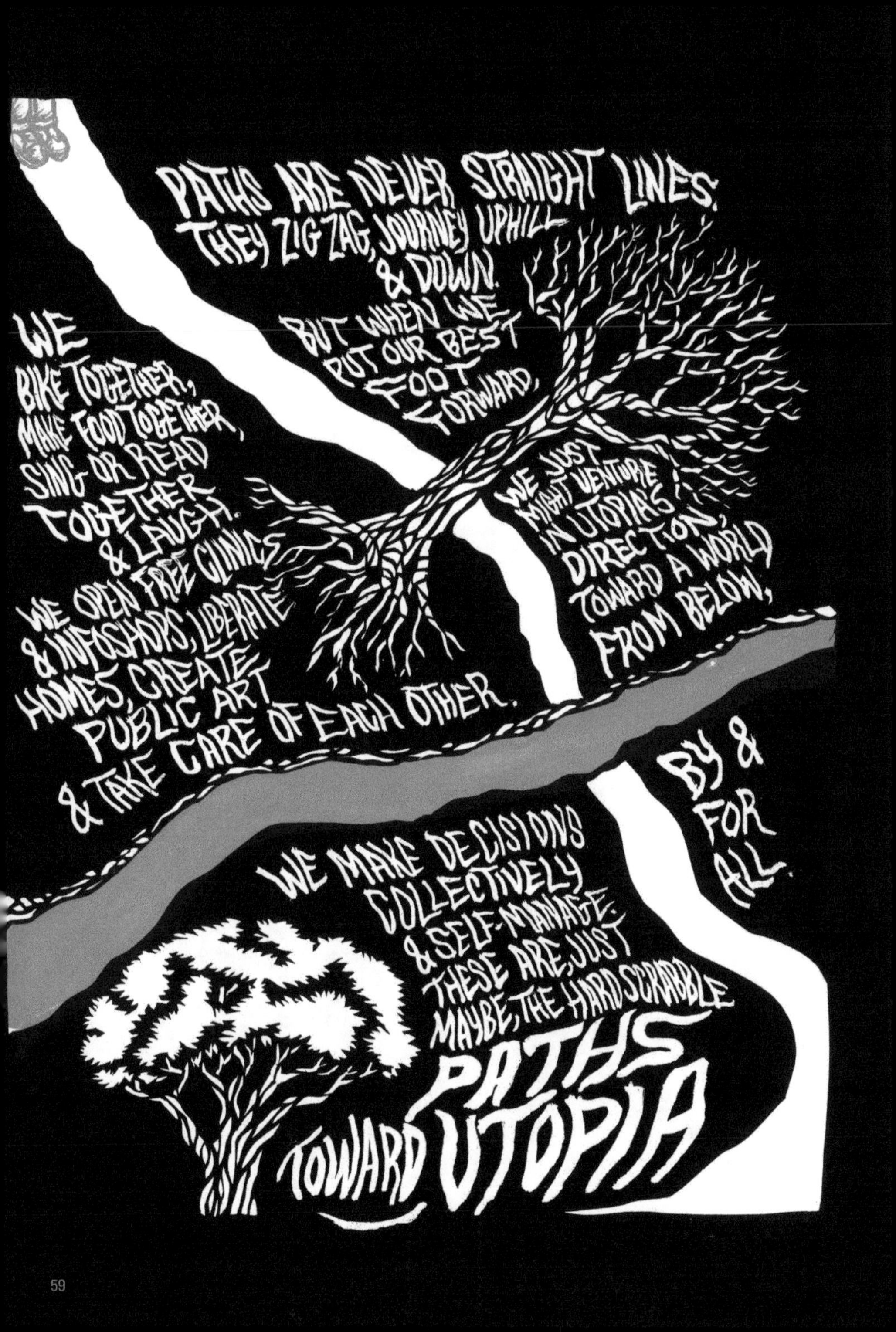
PATHS ARE NEVER STRAIGHT LINES.
THEY ZIG ZAG, JOURNEY UPHILL & DOWN.
BUT WHEN WE PUT OUR BEST FOOT FORWARD,
WE JUST MIGHT VENTURE IN UTOPIA'S DIRECTION, TOWARD A WORLD FROM BELOW,
WE BIKE TOGETHER, MAKE FOOD TOGETHER, SING OR READ TOGETHER & LAUGH.
WE OPEN FREE CLINICS & INFOSHOPS, LIBERATE HOMES, CREATE PUBLIC ART & TAKE CARE OF EACH OTHER.
BY & FOR ALL.
WE MAKE DECISIONS COLLECTIVELY & SELF-MANAGE.
THESE ARE, JUST MAYBE, THE HARD SCRABBLE
PATHS TOWARD UTOPIA

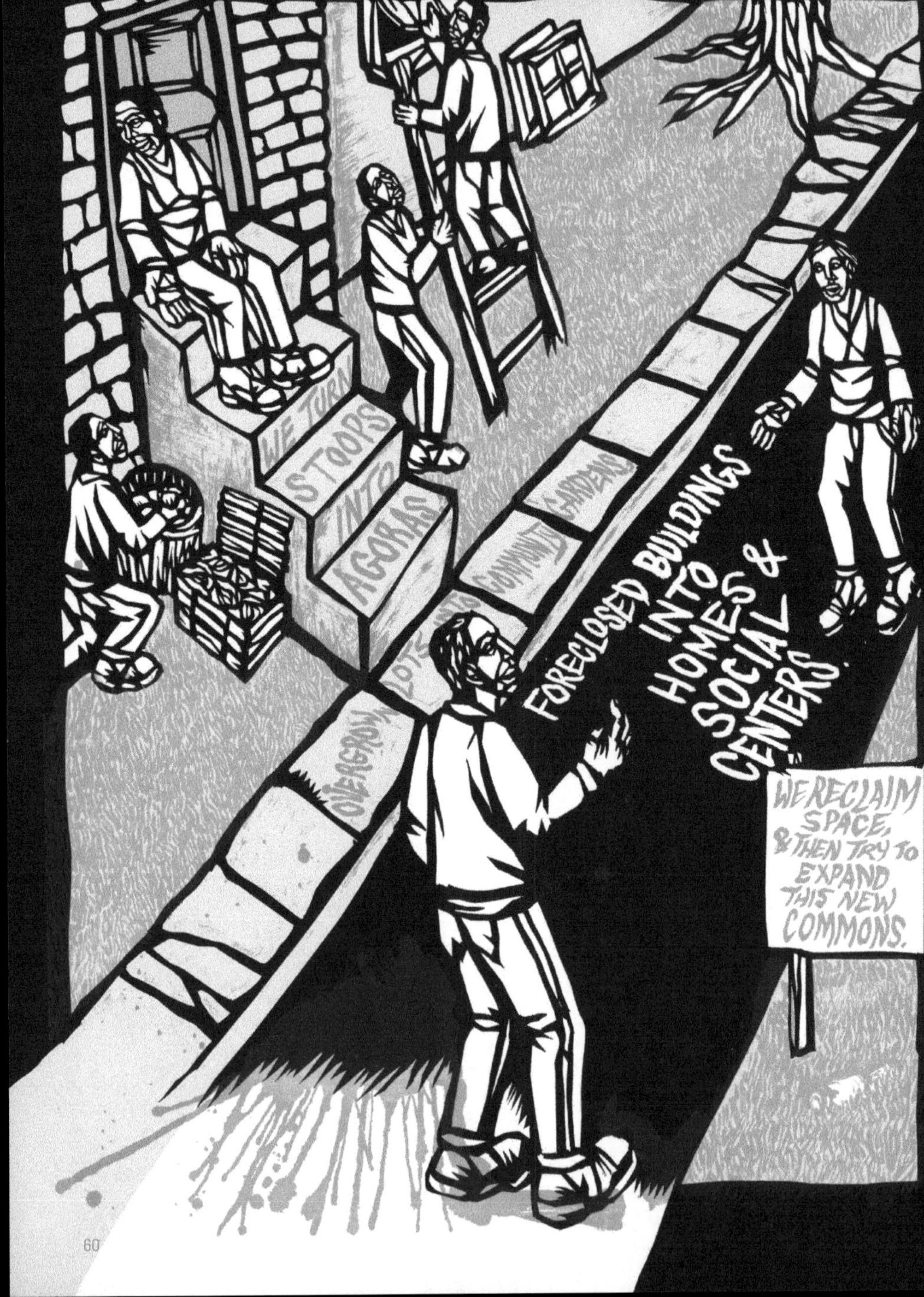
WE TURN STOOPS INTO AGORAS
OVERGROWN LOTS INTO COMMUNITY GARDENS
FORECLOSED BUILDINGS INTO HOMES & SOCIAL CENTERS.
WE RECLAIM SPACE, & THEN TRY TO EXPAND THIS NEW COMMONS.

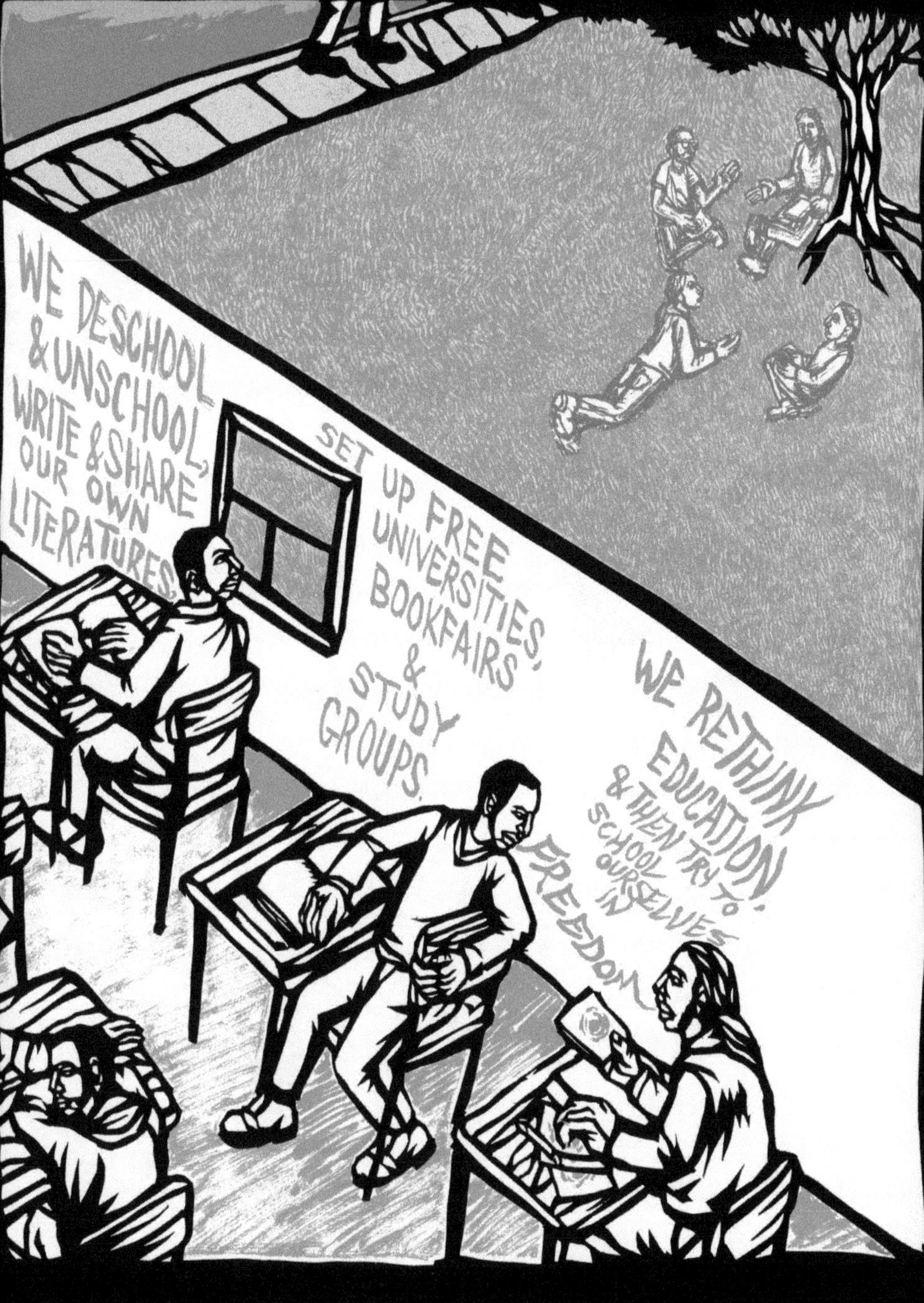
WE DESCHOOL & UNSCHOOL, WRITE & SHARE OUR OWN LITERATURES,
SET UP FREE UNIVERSITIES, BOOKFAIRS & STUDY GROUPS.
WE RETHINK EDUCATION! & THEN TRY TO SCHOOL OURSELVES IN FREEDOM

WE SOCIALIZE CREATIVITY,
UNCOUPLE ART FROM COMMERCE,
EXPERIMENT WITH DO-IT-OURSELVES CULTURE.
WE REAPPROPRIATE THE IMAGINATION,
& THEN TRY TO MAKE OUR ETHICAL YEARNINGS INTO LIVED REALITIES.

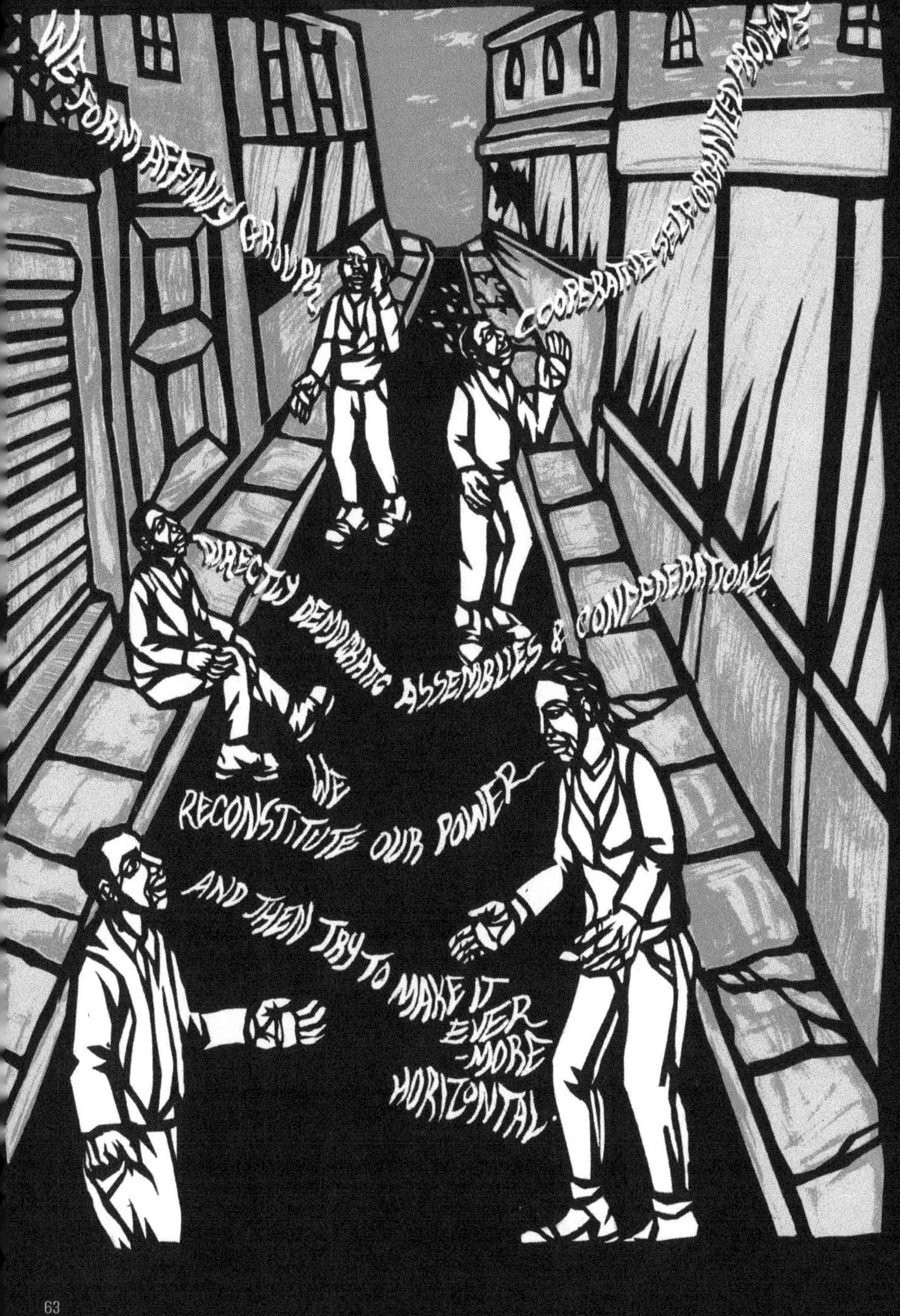
WE FORM AFFINITY GROUPS,
COOPERATIVE SELF-ORGANIZED PROJECTS,
DIRECTLY DEMOCRATIC ASSEMBLIES & CONFEDERATIONS.
WE RECONSTITUTE OUR POWER—
AND THEN TRY TO MAKE IT EVER-MORE HORIZONTAL.

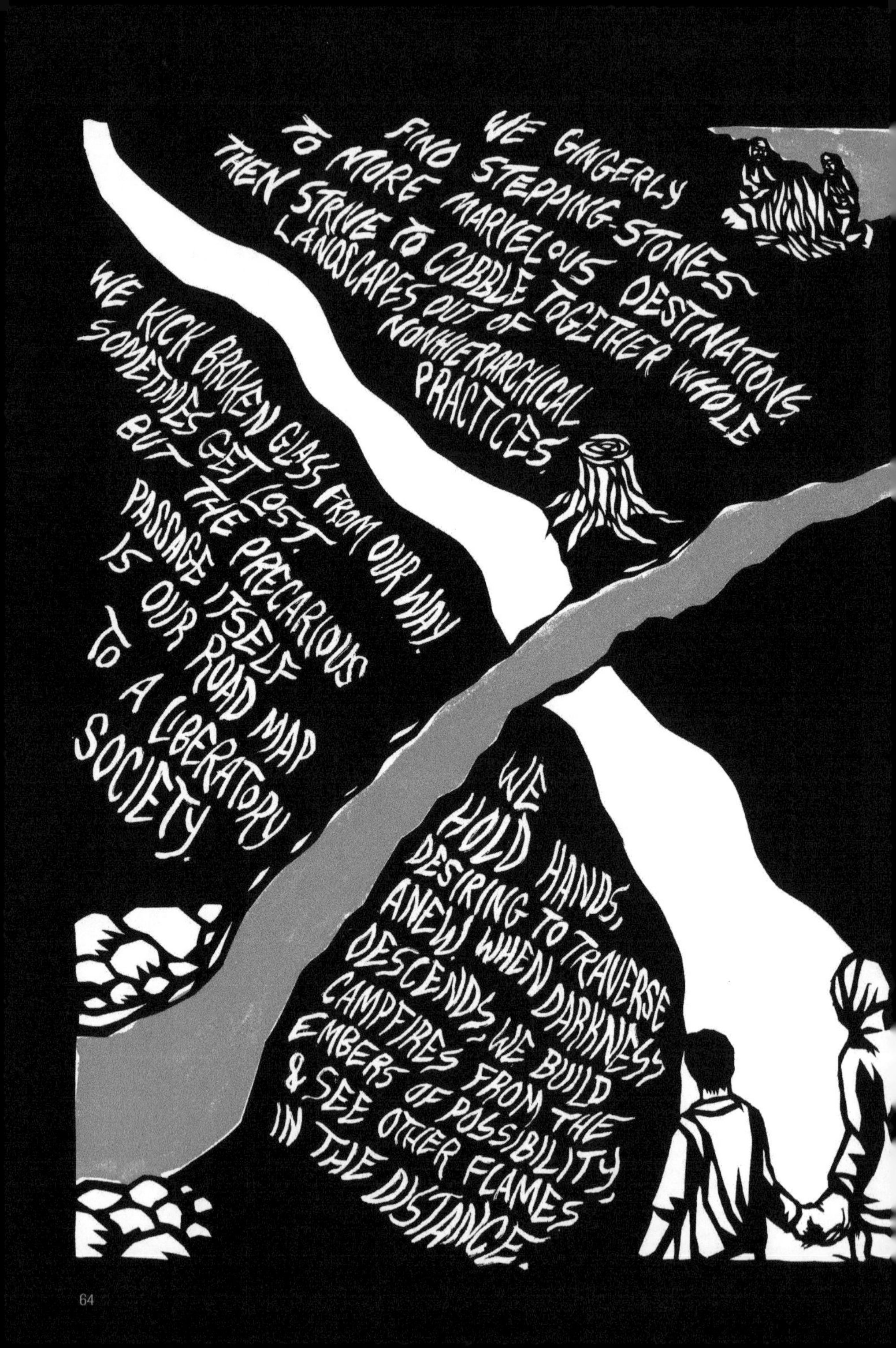
WE GINGERLY
FIND STEPPING-STONES
TO MORE MARVELOUS DESTINATIONS.
THEN STRIVE TO COBBLE TOGETHER WHOLE
LANDSCAPES OUT OF
NONHIERARCHICAL
PRACTICES.
WE KICK BROKEN GLASS FROM OUR WAY.
SOMETIMES GET LOST.
BUT THE PRECARIOUS
PASSAGE ITSELF
IS OUR ROAD MAP
TO A LIBERATORY
SOCIETY.
WE
HOLD HANDS,
DESIRING TO TRAVERSE
ANEW. WHEN DARKNESS
DESCENDS, WE BUILD
CAMPFIRES FROM THE
EMBERS OF POSSIBILITY,
& SEE OTHER FLAMES
IN THE DISTANCE.

THE GIFT

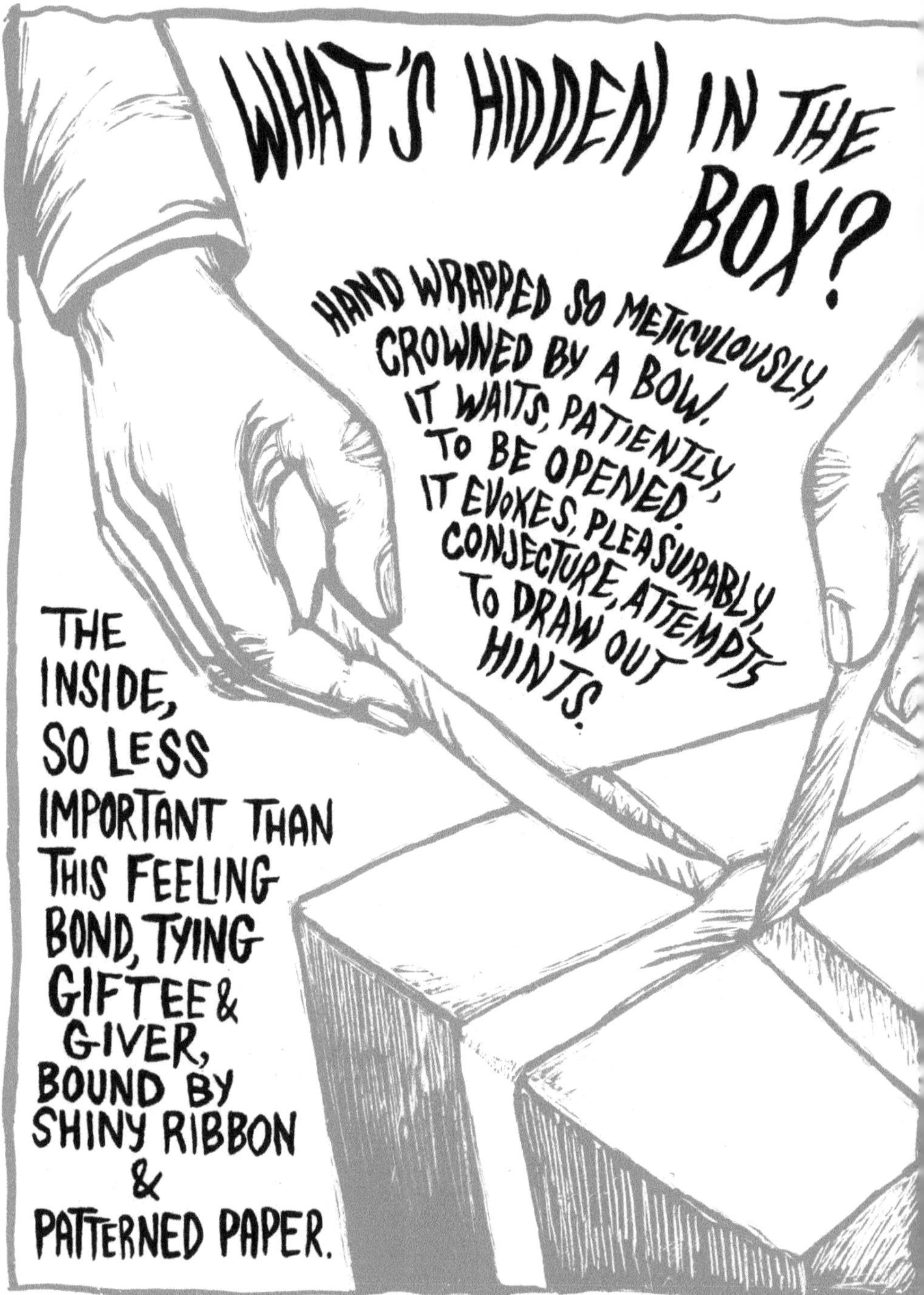
WHAT'S HIDDEN IN THE BOX?
HAND WRAPPED SO METICULOUSLY, CROWNED BY A BOW. IT WAITS, PATIENTLY, TO BE OPENED. IT EVOKES, PLEASURABLY, CONJECTURE, ATTEMPTS TO DRAW OUT HINTS.
THE INSIDE, SO LESS IMPORTANT THAN THIS FEELING BOND, TYING GIFTEE & GIVER, BOUND BY SHINY RIBBON & PATTERNED PAPER.

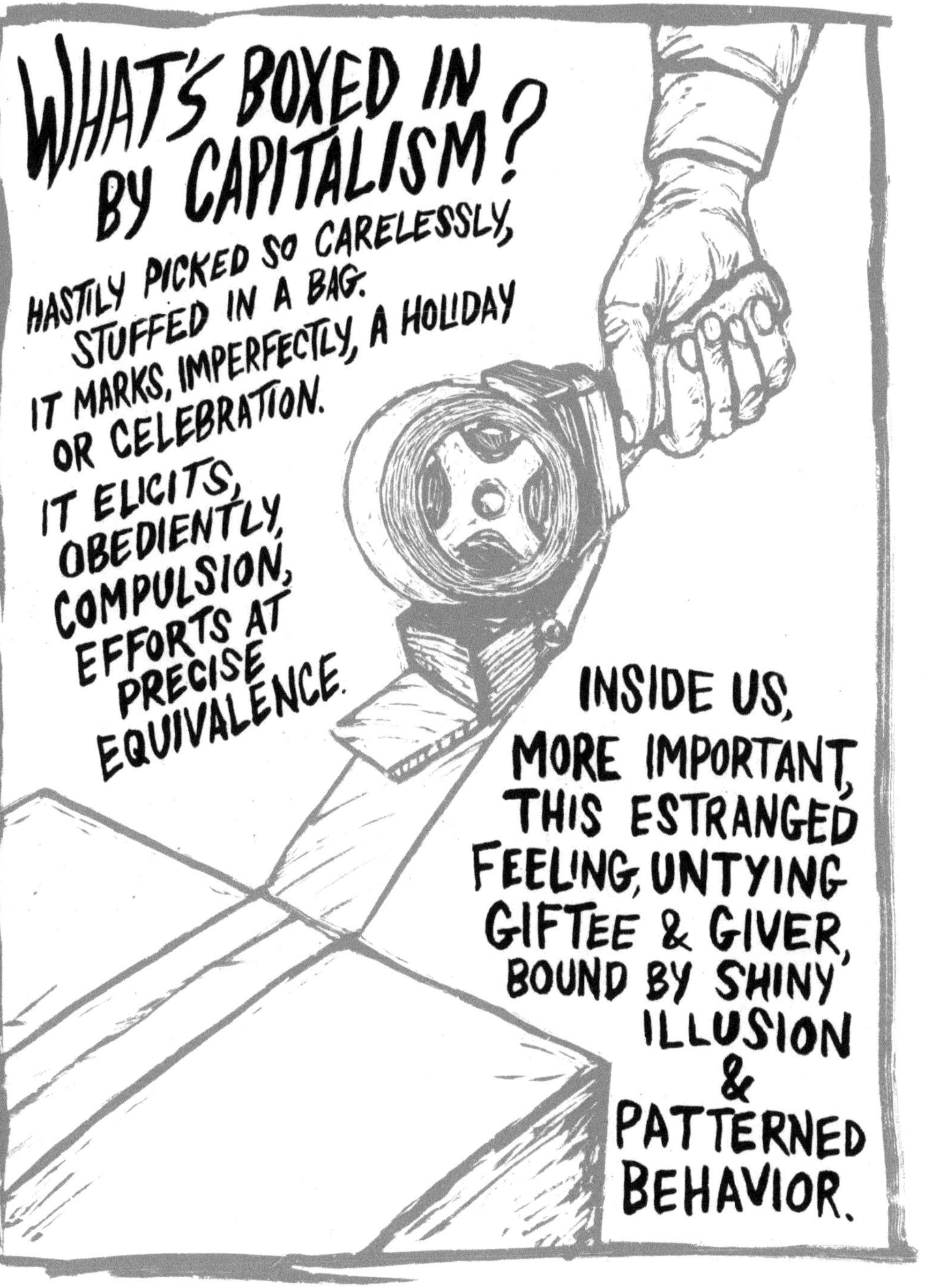
WHAT'S BOXED IN BY CAPITALISM?
HASTILY PICKED SO CARELESSLY, STUFFED IN A BAG.
IT MARKS, IMPERFECTLY, A HOLIDAY OR CELEBRATION.
IT ELICITS, OBEDIENTLY, COMPULSION, EFFORTS AT PRECISE EQUIVALENCE.
INSIDE US, MORE IMPORTANT, THIS ESTRANGED FEELING, UNTYING GIFTEE & GIVER, BOUND BY SHINY ILLUSION & PATTERNED BEHAVIOR.

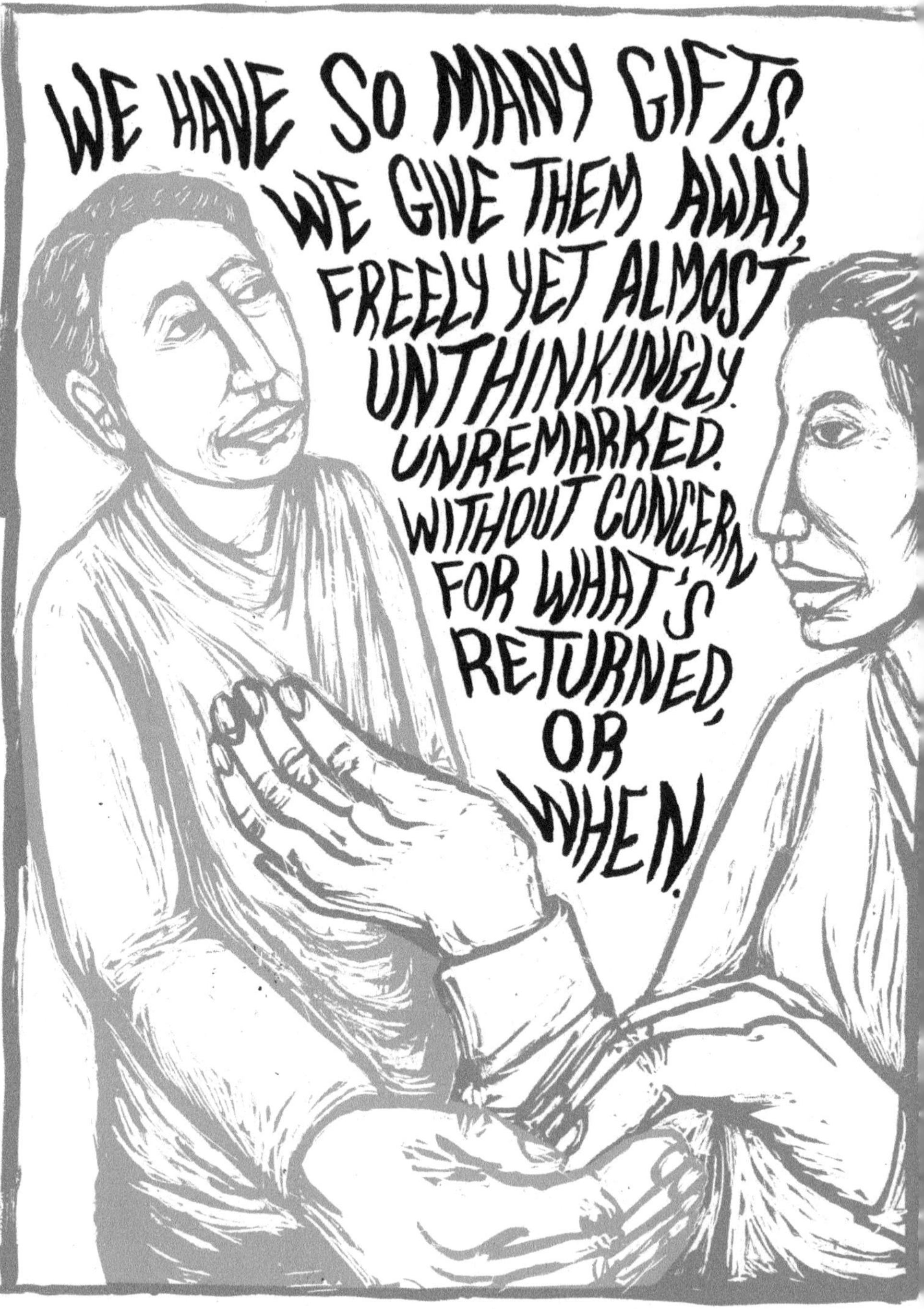
WE HAVE SO MANY GIFTS.
WE GIVE THEM AWAY,
FREELY YET ALMOST
UNTHINKINGLY.
UNREMARKED.
WITHOUT CONCERN
FOR WHAT'S
RETURNED,
OR
WHEN.

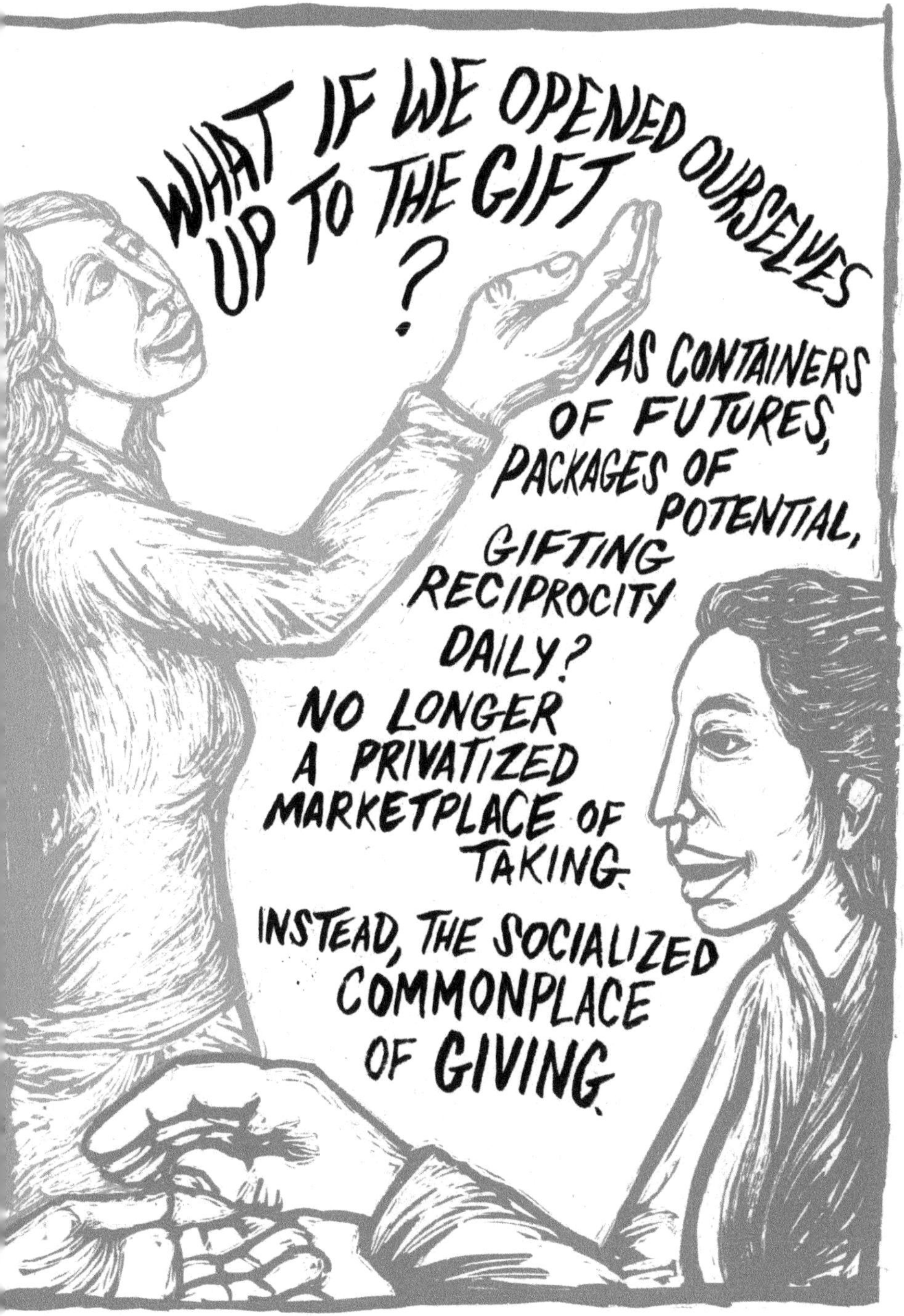
WHAT IF WE OPENED OURSELVES UP TO THE GIFT ?
AS CONTAINERS OF FUTURES, PACKAGES OF POTENTIAL, GIFTING RECIPROCITY DAILY?
NO LONGER A PRIVATIZED MARKETPLACE OF TAKING.
INSTEAD, THE SOCIALIZED COMMONPLACE OF GIVING.

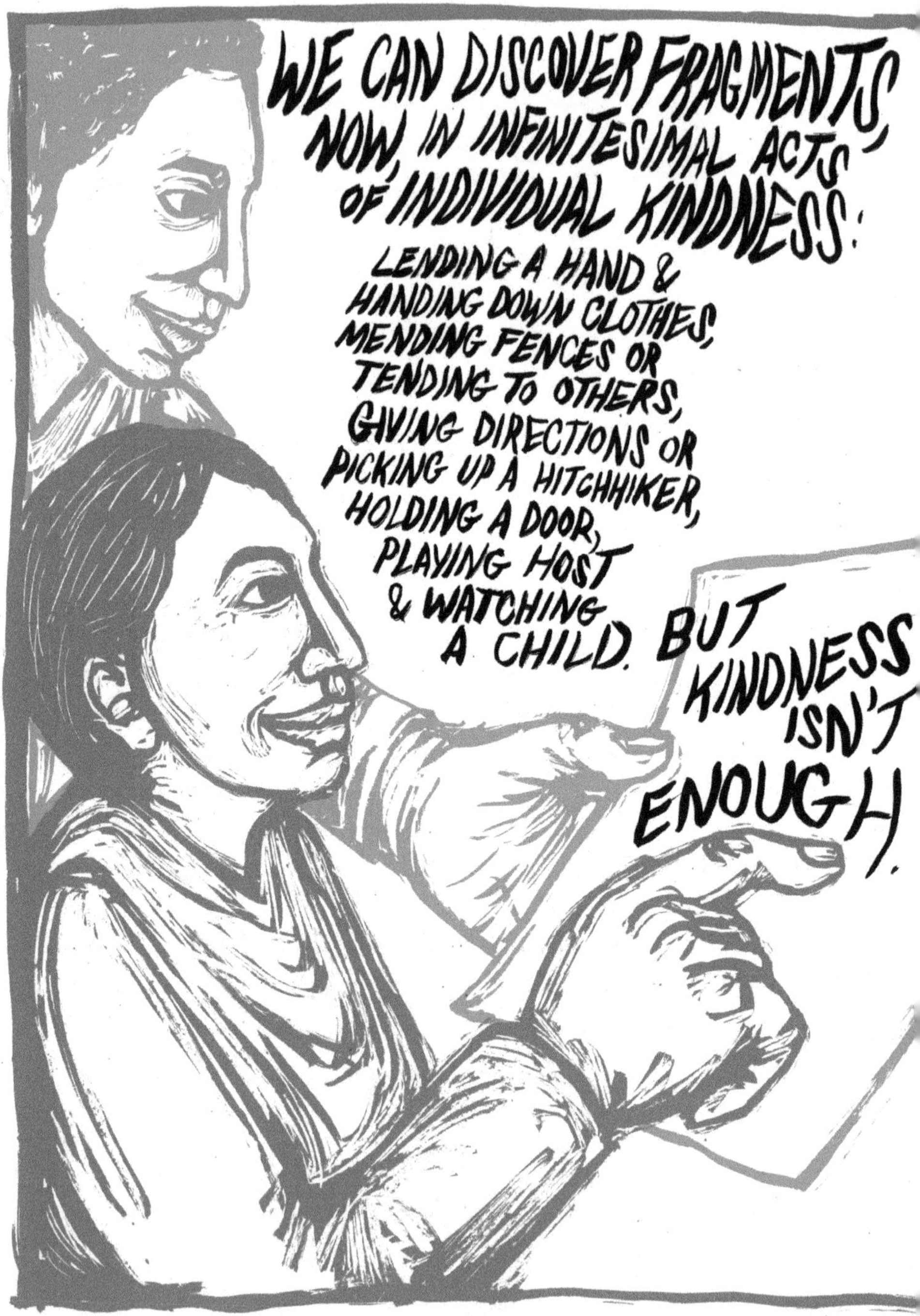
WE CAN DISCOVER FRAGMENTS NOW, IN INFINITESIMAL ACTS OF INDIVIDUAL KINDNESS:
LENDING A HAND & HANDING DOWN CLOTHES, MENDING FENCES OR TENDING TO OTHERS, GIVING DIRECTIONS OR PICKING UP A HITCHHIKER, HOLDING A DOOR, PLAYING HOST & WATCHING A CHILD.
BUT KINDNESS ISN'T ENOUGH.

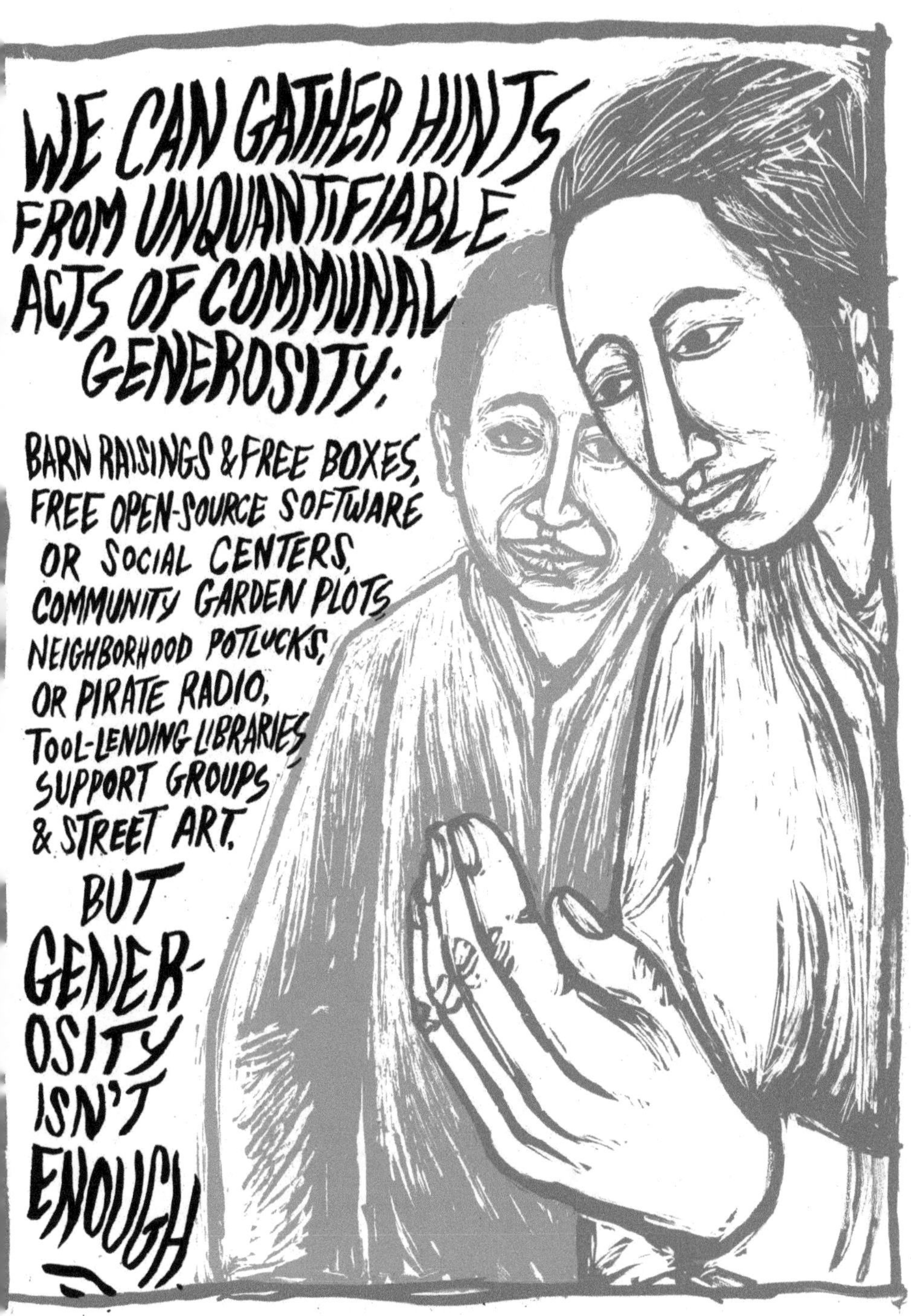
WE CAN GATHER HINTS FROM UNQUANTIFIABLE ACTS OF COMMUNAL GENEROSITY:
BARN RAISINGS & FREE BOXES, FREE OPEN-SOURCE SOFTWARE OR SOCIAL CENTERS, COMMUNITY GARDEN PLOTS, NEIGHBORHOOD POTLUCKS, OR PIRATE RADIO, TOOL-LENDING LIBRARIES, SUPPORT GROUPS & STREET ART.
BUT GENER-OSITY ISN'T ENOUGH.

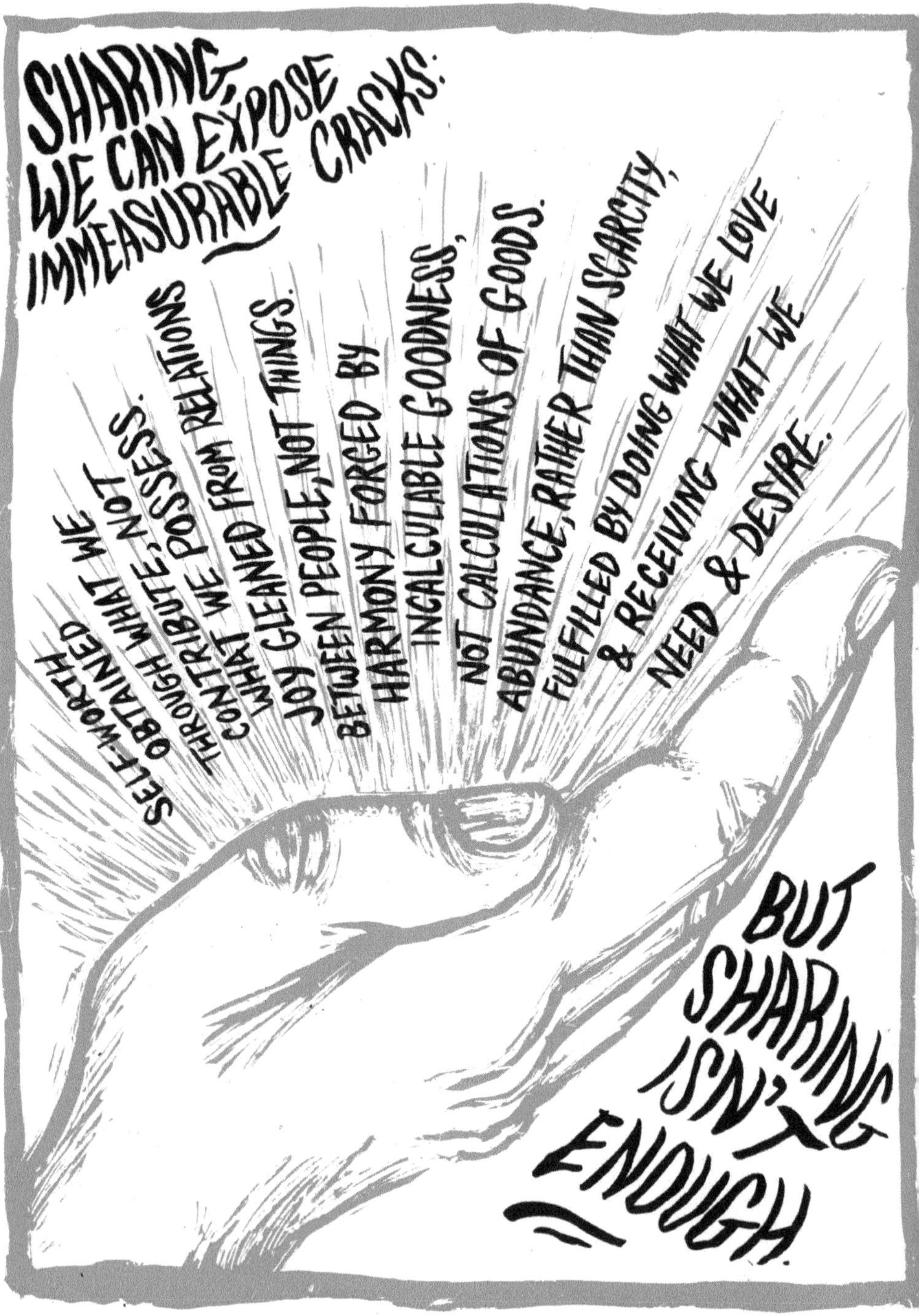
SHARING, WE CAN EXPOSE IMMEASURABLE CRACKS:
SELF-WORTH OBTAINED THROUGH WHAT WE CONTRIBUTE, NOT WHAT WE POSSESS.
JOY GLEANED FROM RELATIONS BETWEEN PEOPLE, NOT THINGS.
HARMONY FORGED BY INCALCULABLE GOODNESS, NOT CALCULATIONS OF GOODS.
ABUNDANCE, RATHER THAN SCARCITY, FULFILLED BY DOING WHAT WE LOVE & RECEIVING WHAT WE NEED & DESIRE.
BUT SHARING ISN'T ENOUGH.

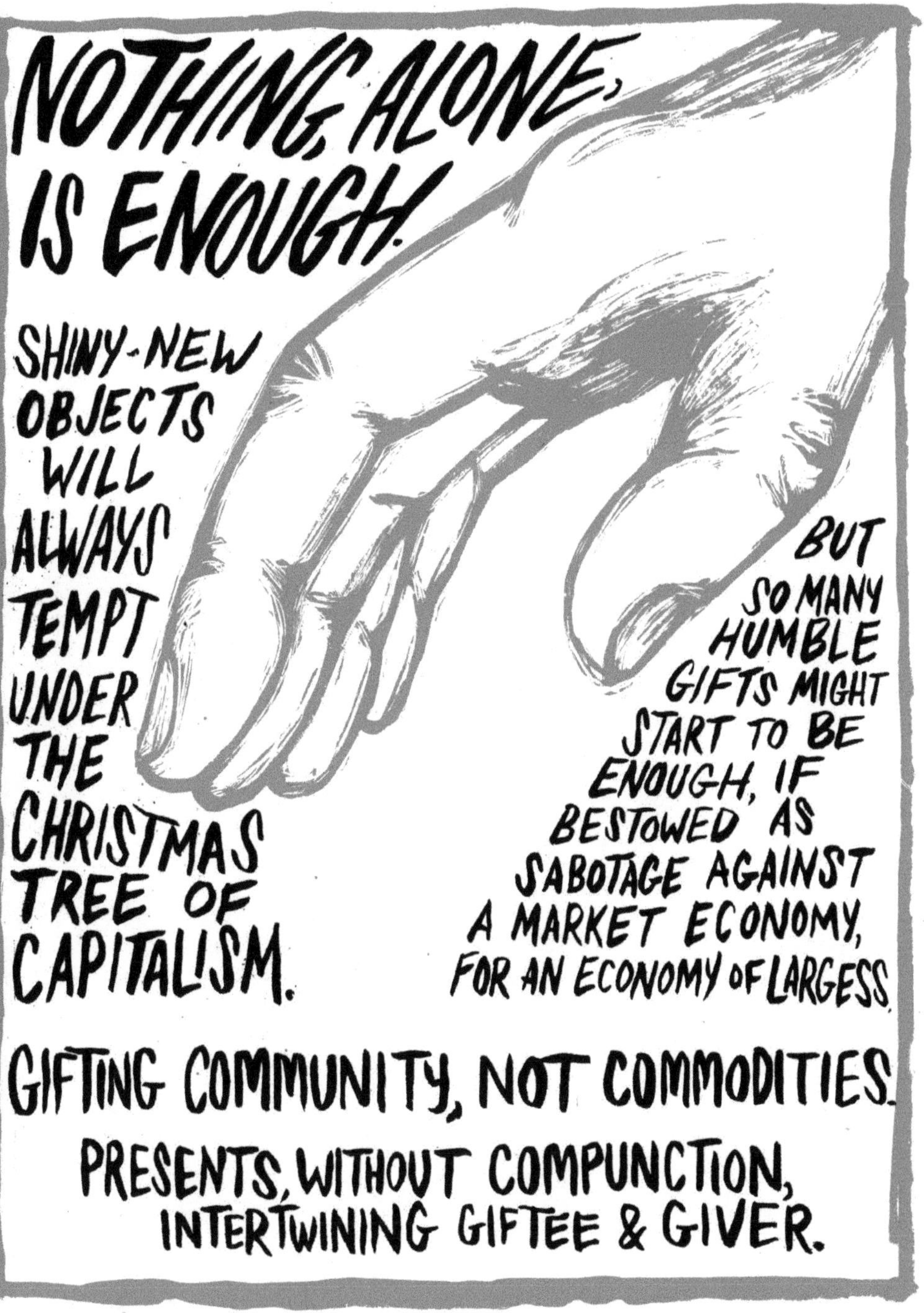
NOTHING, ALONE, IS ENOUGH.
SHINY-NEW OBJECTS WILL ALWAYS TEMPT UNDER THE CHRISTMAS TREE OF CAPITALISM.
BUT SO MANY HUMBLE GIFTS MIGHT START TO BE ENOUGH, IF BESTOWED AS SABOTAGE AGAINST A MARKET ECONOMY, FOR AN ECONOMY OF LARGESS.
GIFTING COMMUNITY, NOT COMMODITIES.
PRESENTS, WITHOUT COMPUNCTION, INTERTWINING GIFTEE & GIVER.

DECIDING FOR OURSELVES

ON THE BLEAK TERRAIN OF A GRAY CITY,
GRAY WITH MISERY & MEMORIES OF DEATH,
WHERE INVISIBLE HANDS DEVISE "NATURAL" DISASTERS,
CONSTRUCTING LEVEES THAT BREAK IN HURRICANES
& NUCLEAR POWER PLANTS THAT MELT IN EARTH-QUAKES,
WHILE OTHER INVISIBLE HANDS
STEAL LAND & ERECT PRISONS,
OR SHUTTER FACTORIES & SCHOOLS,

WHILE STILL MORE INVISIBLE HANDS
PRIVATIZE WATER,
PILING DEVASTATION
ON POOR & MARGINALIZED PEOPLE,
BLACK, INDIGENOUS, FEMALE, QUEER, NON-ENGLISH SPEAKING, ANYONE WHO IS "OTHER"
THE HAGGARD RAINBOW OF HUMANITY, THROWN OUT LIKE SO MUCH TRASH INTO A LANDFILL OF SOCIALLY CONSTRUCTED SORROWS—

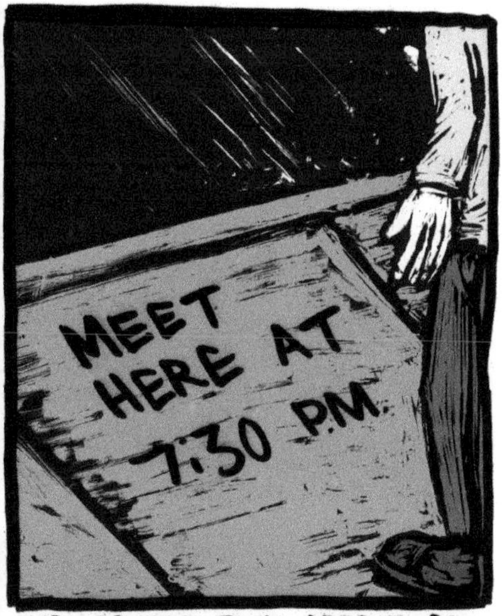
MEET HERE AT 7:30 P.M

NO ONE EVER TOOK CREDIT, BUT ONE MORNING, CHALKED ON THE SIDEWALK, A MESSAGE APPEARED.

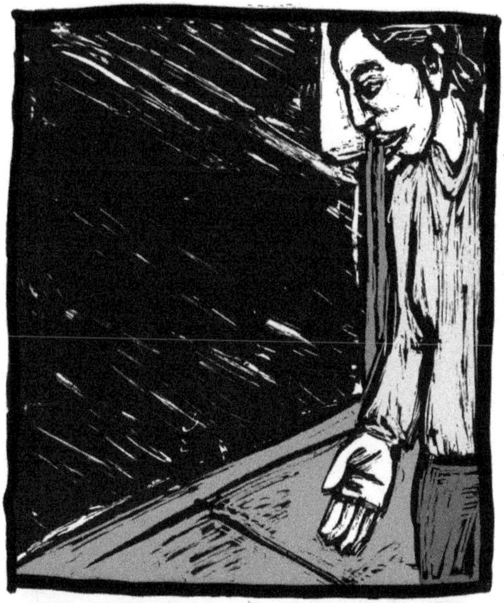

SHE RUBBED THE SLEEP FROM HER EYES TO STARE AT THE NEATLY PRINTED WORDS, HERE ON HER STREET CORNER.

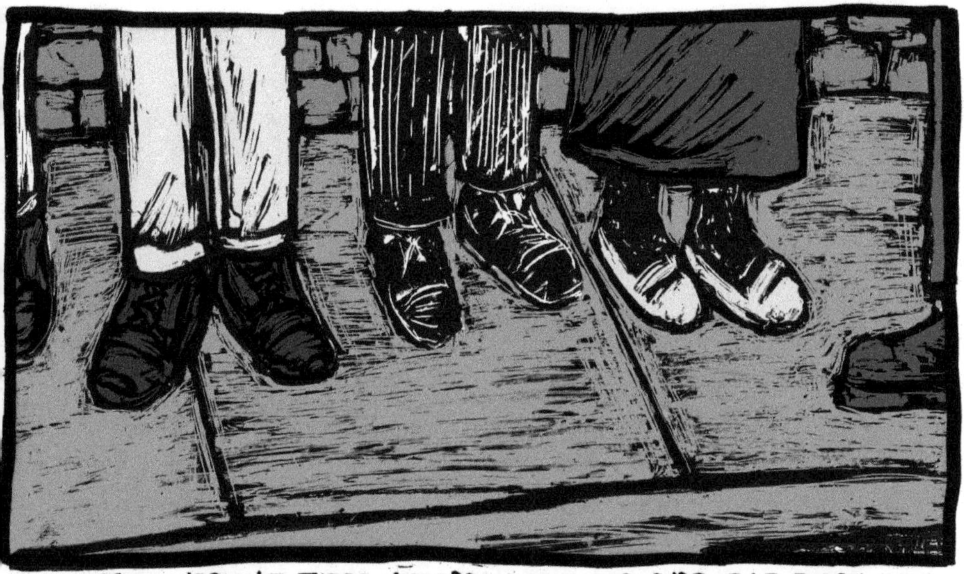

THE LETTERS WEREN'T THERE YESTERDAY. SHE WAS SURE OF IT. EVERY DAY, ON HER WAY TO WORK, THIS SLAB OF PAVEMENT WAS HER BUS STOP. SHE ALWAYS LOOKED DOWN, WAITING SILENTLY AMONG STRANGERS, MEMORIZING THE GRAY CONCRETE PATCH, THEN SILENTLY RIDING TO HER GRAY OFFICE.

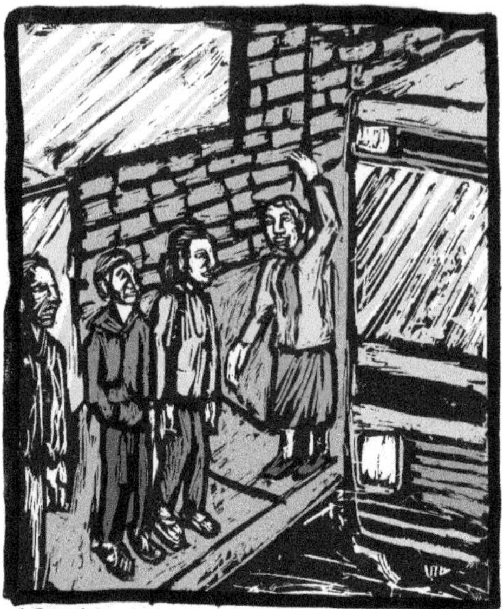

"THEY'VE SHUT ALL THE BANKS!" A FRANTIC VOICE EXCLAIMED BEHIND HER. SHE RUBBED HER EYES AGAIN & THEN WIDENED THEM. THE BUS PULLED UP, WHEEZING TO A HALT.

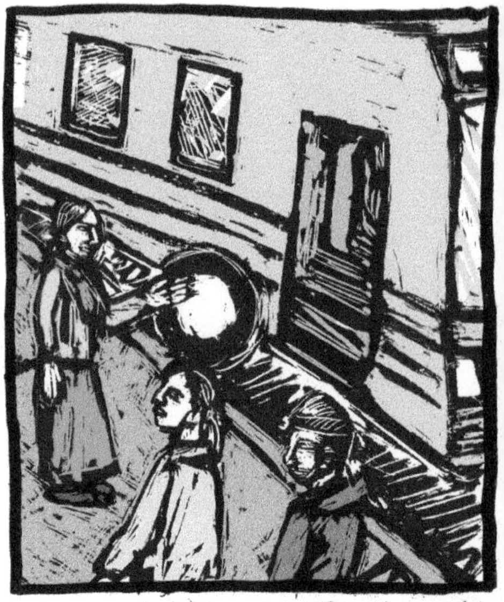

"COME ON, LET'S GO DOWNTOWN. I HEAR PEOPLE ARE SMASHING ATMS!" THIS STRANGER, HER NEIGHBOR WHO NEVER SAID HELLO, SMILED. THE DRIVER SMILED TOO: "NO CHARGE TODAY."

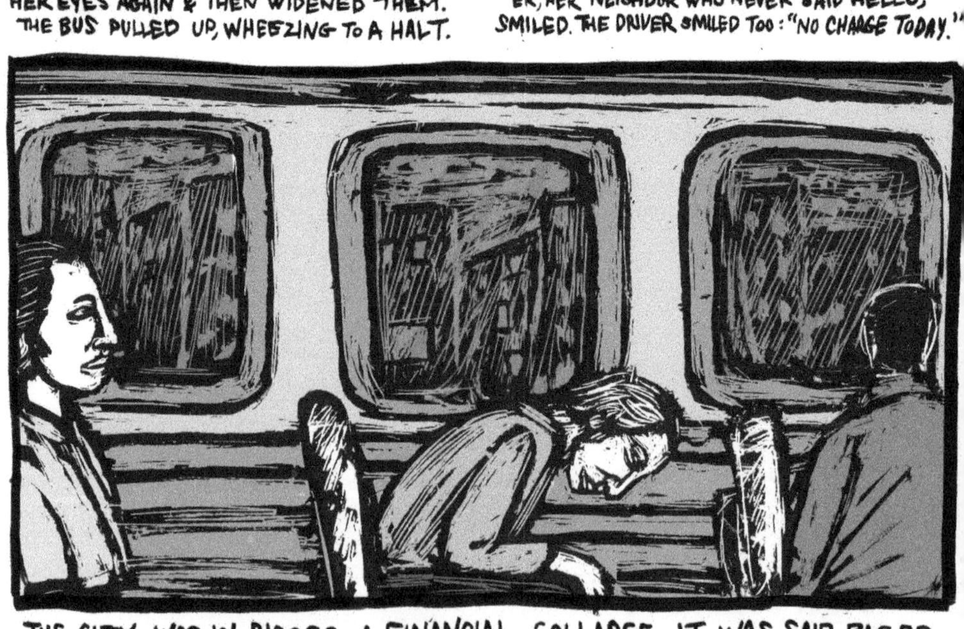

THE CITY WAS IN PIECES. A FINANCIAL COLLAPSE, IT WAS SAID, BASED ON FEARS OF AN ECOLOGICAL COLLAPSE. SHE KNEW THE METROPOLE WAS ALREADY IN TATTERS. IN HER NEIGHBORHOOD, THERE WAS PLENTY OF NOTHING.

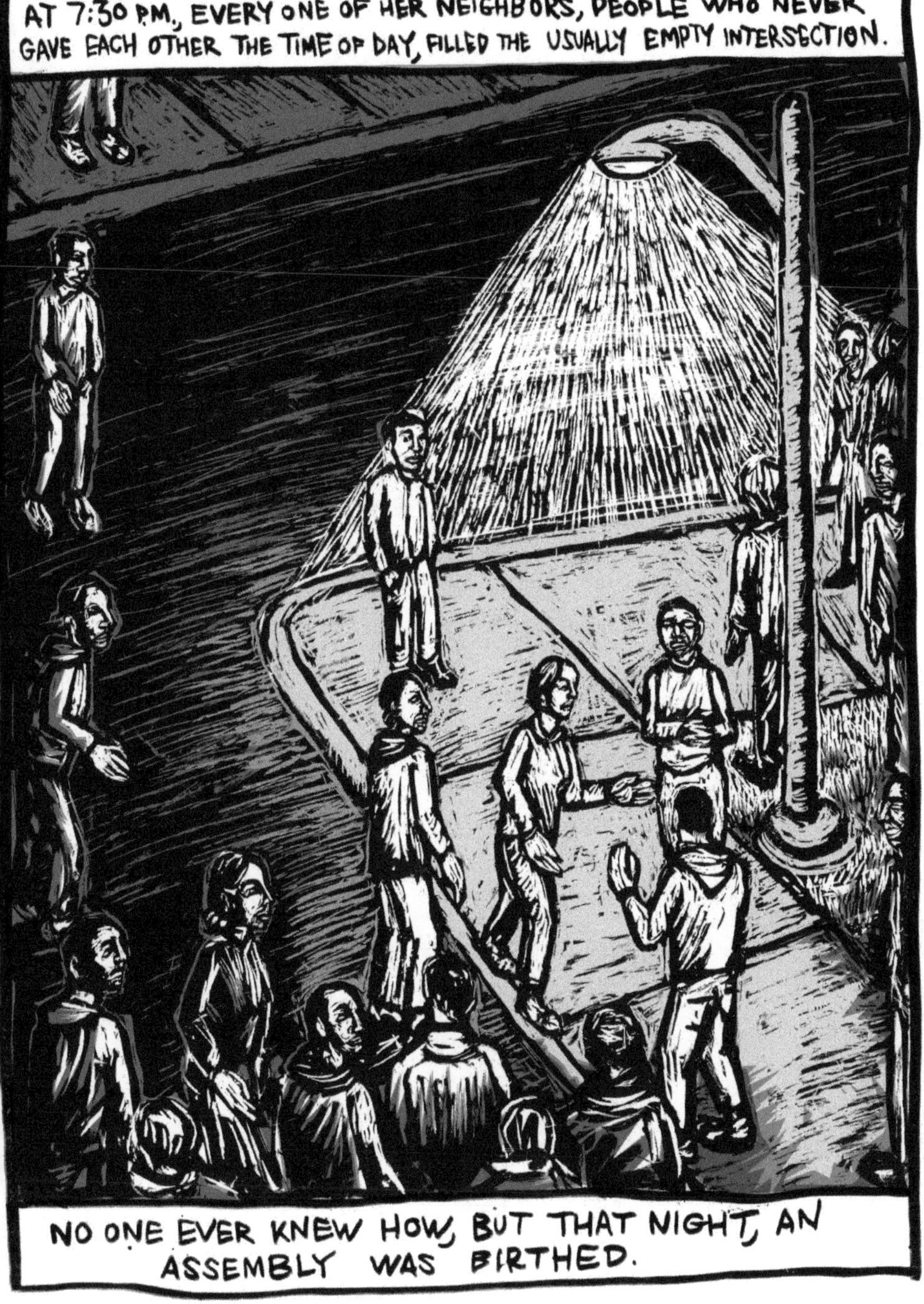
AT 7:30 P.M., EVERY ONE OF HER NEIGHBORS, PEOPLE WHO NEVER GAVE EACH OTHER THE TIME OF DAY, FILLED THE USUALLY EMPTY INTERSECTION.
NO ONE EVER KNEW HOW, BUT THAT NIGHT, AN ASSEMBLY WAS BIRTHED.

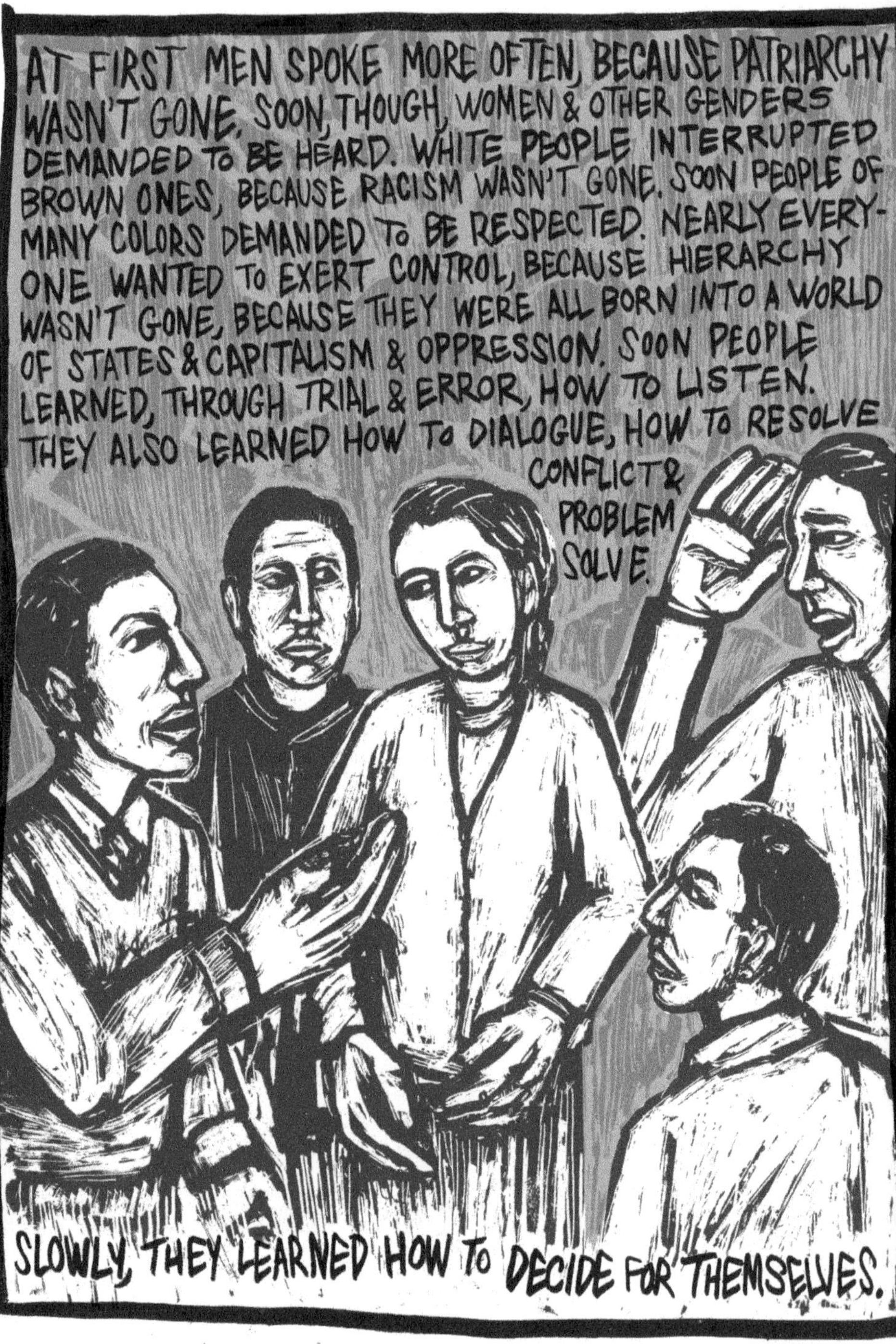
AT FIRST MEN SPOKE MORE OFTEN, BECAUSE PATRIARCHY WASN'T GONE. SOON, THOUGH, WOMEN & OTHER GENDERS DEMANDED TO BE HEARD. WHITE PEOPLE INTERRUPTED BROWN ONES, BECAUSE RACISM WASN'T GONE. SOON PEOPLE OF MANY COLORS DEMANDED TO BE RESPECTED. NEARLY EVERYONE WANTED TO EXERT CONTROL, BECAUSE HIERARCHY WASN'T GONE, BECAUSE THEY WERE ALL BORN INTO A WORLD OF STATES & CAPITALISM & OPPRESSION. SOON PEOPLE LEARNED, THROUGH TRIAL & ERROR, HOW TO LISTEN. THEY ALSO LEARNED HOW TO DIALOGUE, HOW TO RESOLVE CONFLICT & PROBLEM SOLVE.
SLOWLY, THEY LEARNED HOW TO DECIDE FOR THEMSELVES.

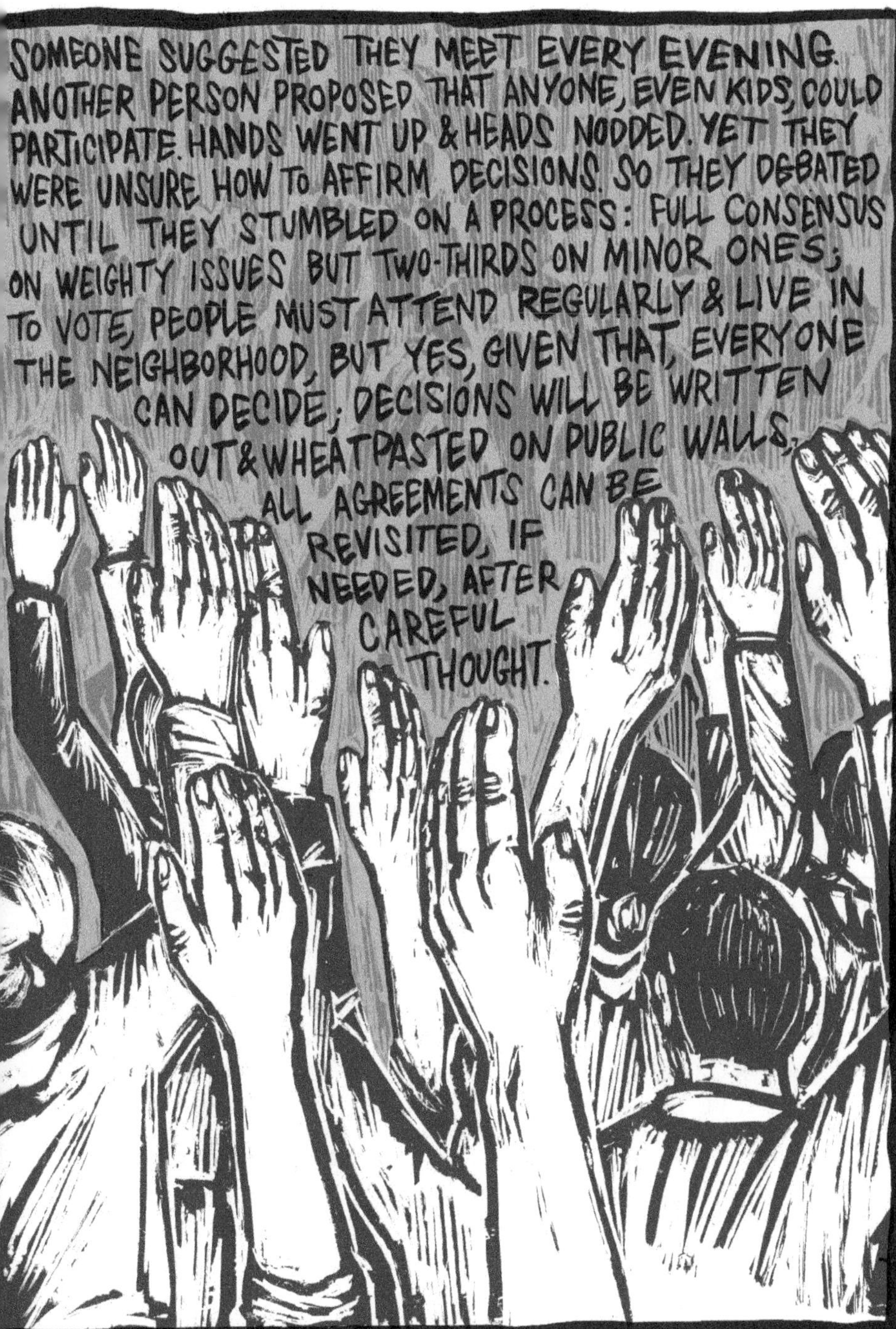

SOMEONE SUGGESTED THEY MEET EVERY EVENING. ANOTHER PERSON PROPOSED THAT ANYONE, EVEN KIDS, COULD PARTICIPATE. HANDS WENT UP & HEADS NODDED. YET THEY WERE UNSURE HOW TO AFFIRM DECISIONS. SO THEY DEBATED UNTIL THEY STUMBLED ON A PROCESS: FULL CONSENSUS ON WEIGHTY ISSUES BUT TWO-THIRDS ON MINOR ONES; TO VOTE, PEOPLE MUST ATTEND REGULARLY & LIVE IN THE NEIGHBORHOOD, BUT YES, GIVEN THAT, EVERYONE CAN DECIDE; DECISIONS WILL BE WRITTEN OUT & WHEATPASTED ON PUBLIC WALLS; ALL AGREEMENTS CAN BE REVISITED, IF NEEDED, AFTER CAREFUL THOUGHT.

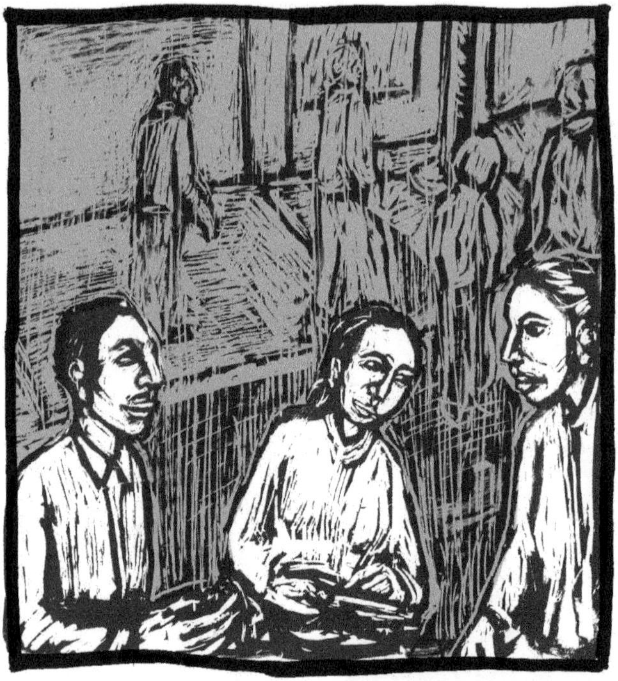

OVER TIME, PEOPLE INCREASINGLY FOUND COMMON GROUND. THEY CAME TO KNOW & TRUST EACH OTHER, SO DECISIONS SEEMED EASIER. THE ASSEMBLY BECAME MORE EFFICIENT & MEETINGS WERE SHORTER. WORKING COMMITTEES ACCOUNTABLE TO THE NIGHTLY BODY, WERE SET UP.

THE NEIGHBORHOOD, THE NEIGHBORS, CAME ALIVE. OTHER NEIGHBORHOODS DID THE SAME. NO ONE EVER RECOLLECTED HOW, BUT EFFORTLESSLY, COOPERATION BETWEEN DISTRICTS EMERGED.

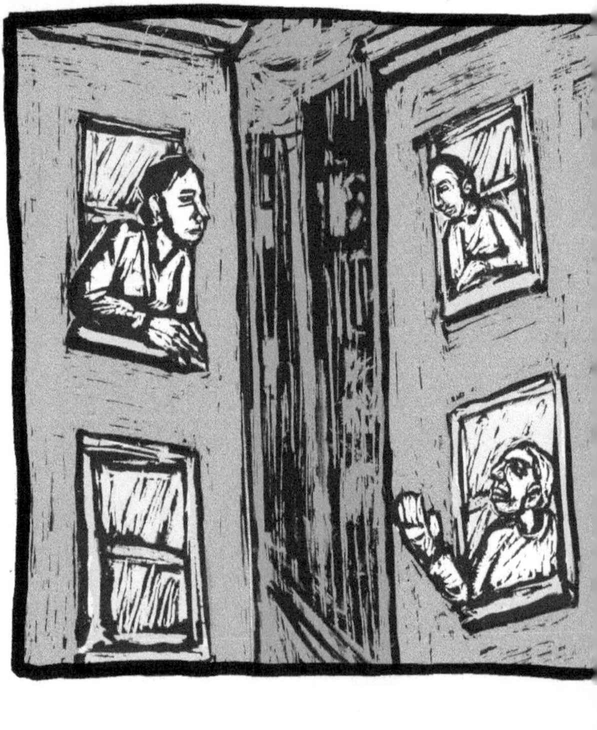

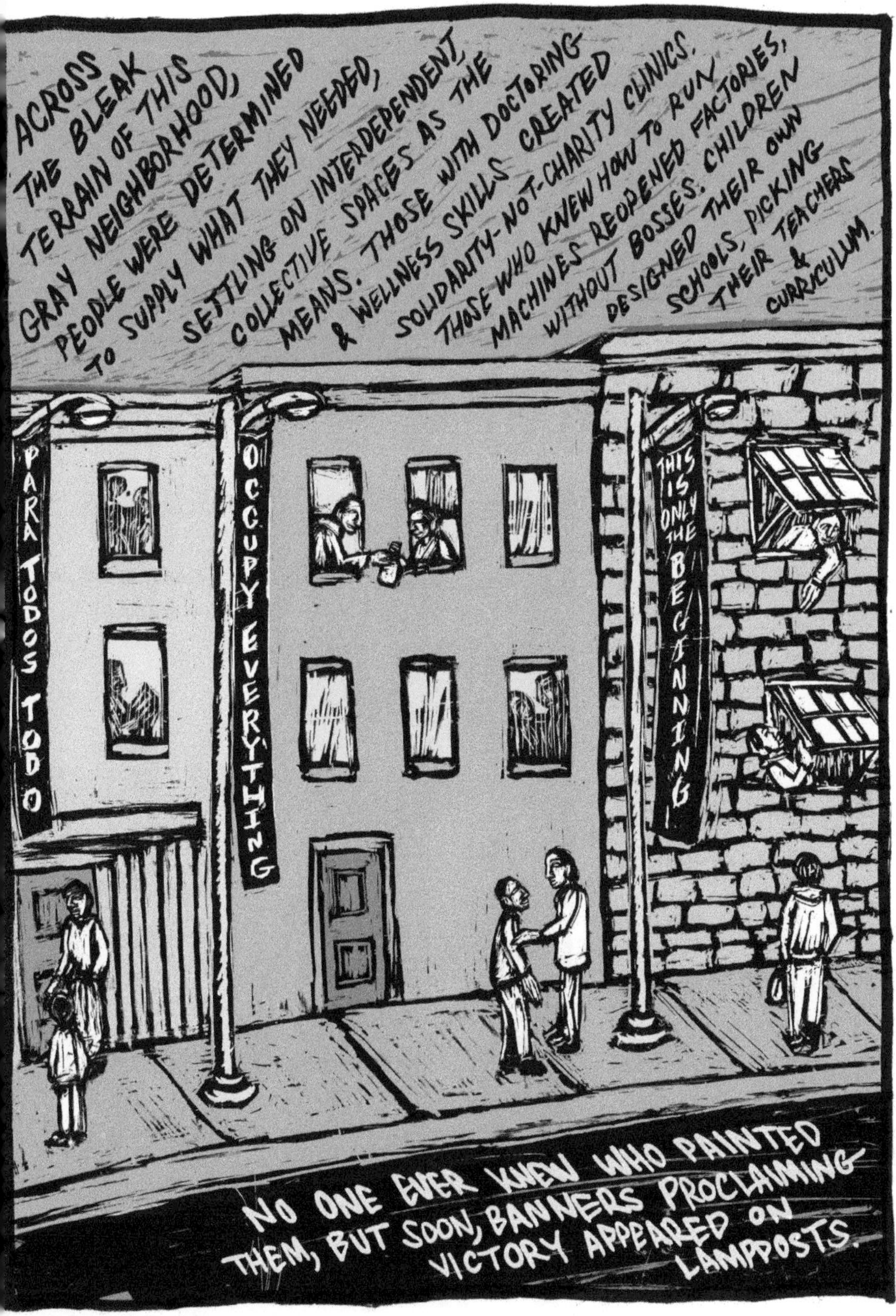
ACROSS THE BLEAK GRAY TERRAIN OF THIS NEIGHBORHOOD, PEOPLE WERE DETERMINED TO SUPPLY WHAT THEY NEEDED, SETTLING ON INTERDEPENDENT, COLLECTIVE SPACES AS THE MEANS. THOSE WITH DOCTORING & WELLNESS SKILLS CREATED SOLIDARITY-NOT-CHARITY CLINICS. THOSE WHO KNEW HOW TO RUN MACHINES REOPENED FACTORIES, WITHOUT BOSSES. CHILDREN DESIGNED THEIR OWN SCHOOLS, PICKING THEIR TEACHERS & CURRICULUM.
PARA TODOS TODO
OCCUPY EVERYTHING
THIS IS ONLY THE BEGINNING
NO ONE EVER KNEW WHO PAINTED THEM, BUT SOON, BANNERS PROCLAIMING VICTORY APPEARED ON LAMPPOSTS.

LOOKING BACK, A FEW YEARS LATER, LONG AFTER HER & HER NEIGHBORS' ASSEMBLY HAD FIZZLED OUT, SHE WONDERED IF IT HAD BEEN A DREAM. NO ONE EVER GRASPED HOW, BUT IMPERCEPTIBLY, "ORDER" HAD BEEN RESTORED. FINANCIAL MARKETS & POLITICIANS TOOK CHARGE. HIPSTER-PIONEERS MIGRATED INTO THE STILL-DECIMATED CITY. IT HADN'T BEEN A TOTAL BACKSLIDE; LOVELY REMNANTS SURVIVED: THE COLLECTIVE THEATER TROUPE, SQUATTING A FORMER BANK BUILDING, A FEW OF THE BLOCK-BY-BLOCK BARTER NETWORKS & THE HARDY POSSE OF FREE PEDICABS. STILL, SHE WONDERED WHY MANY OF HER NEIGHBORS HAD ABANDONED SELF-GOVERNANCE, FALLING AGAIN UNDER THE SWAY OF "COMFORTABLE," PASSIVE COMPLIANCE.

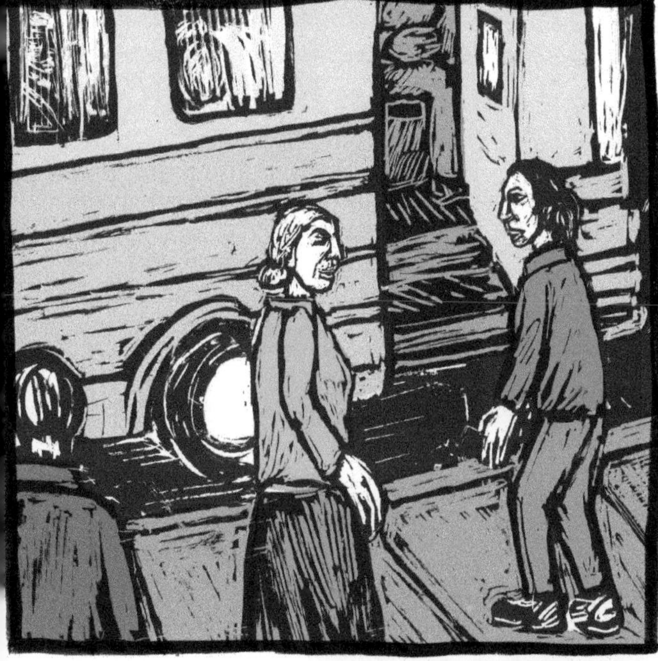

ONE GRAY MONDAY AT HER BUS STOP, HER NEIGHBOR WHO NOW ALWAYS SAID HELLO PAUSED BEFORE BOARDING TO ADD,

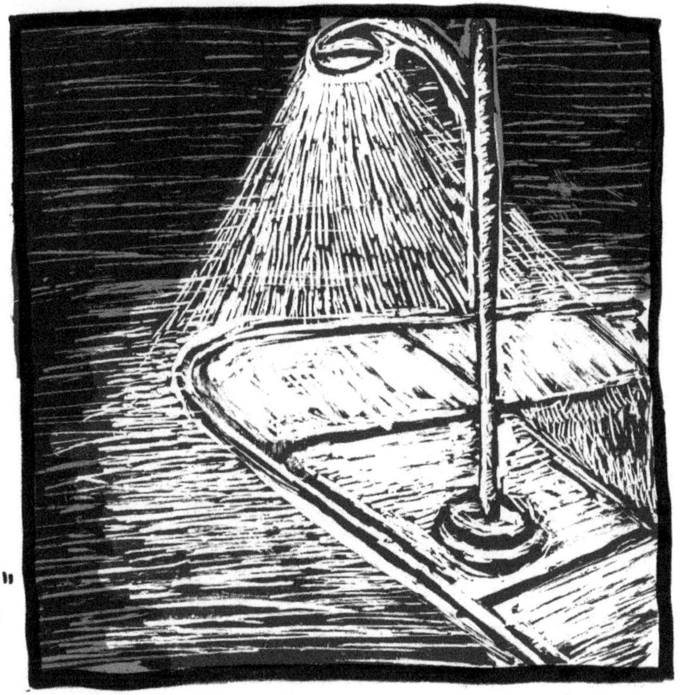

"NO ONE EVER RECALLED HOW, BUT ONE DAY, STATES WERE NO LONGER NATURAL OR NECESSARY. IT'S NOT TOO EARLY TO RECONVENE OUR ASSEMBLY. WHAT DO YOU SAY? TONIGHT AT 7:30?"

WAKING TO REVOLUTION

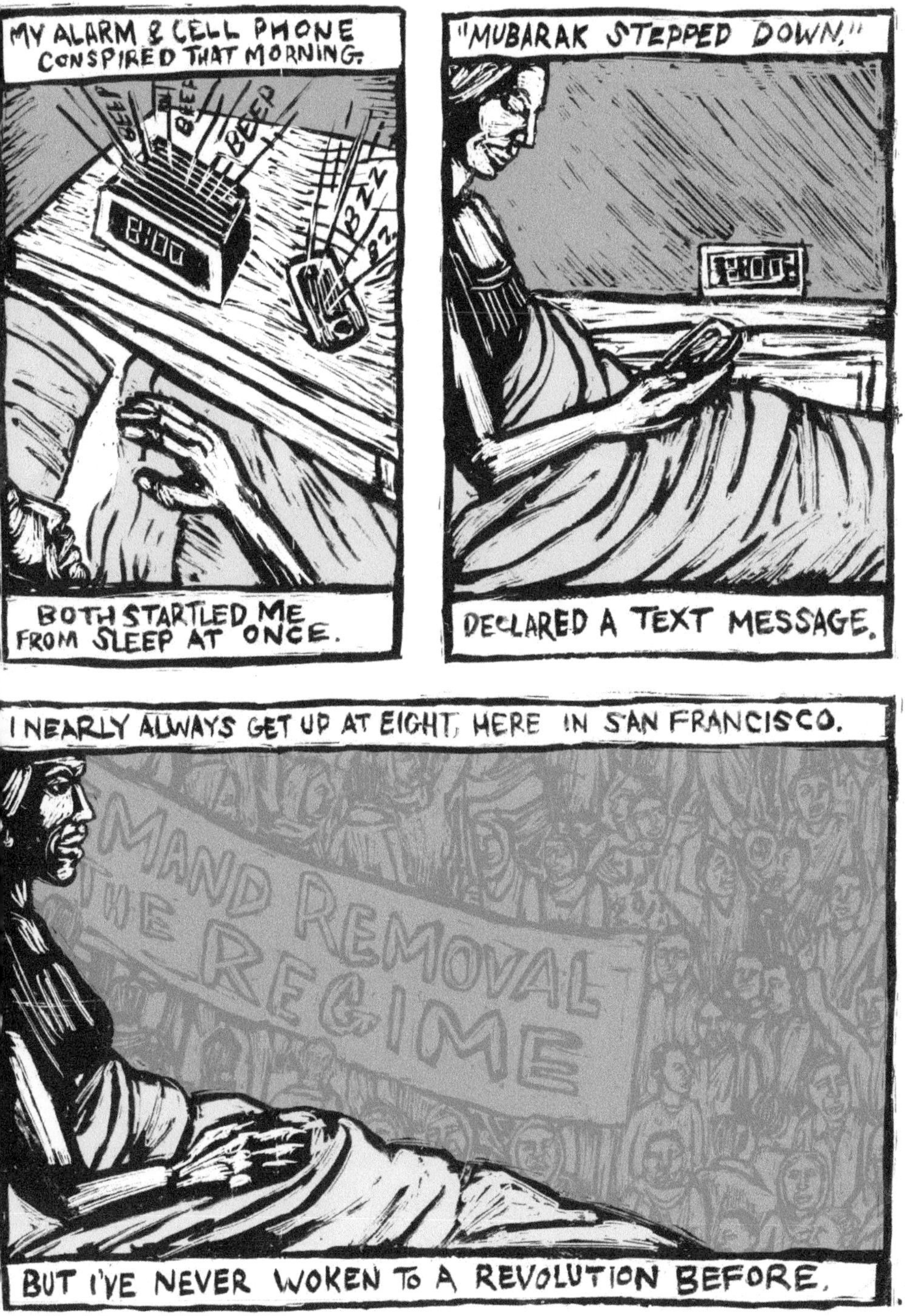
MY ALARM & CELL PHONE CONSPIRED THAT MORNING.
BEEP
BEEP
BEEP
BZZZ
BOTH STARTLED ME FROM SLEEP AT ONCE.
"MUBARAK STEPPED DOWN,"
DECLARED A TEXT MESSAGE.
I NEARLY ALWAYS GET UP AT EIGHT, HERE IN SAN FRANCISCO.
MAND REMOVAL
REGIME
BUT I'VE NEVER WOKEN TO A REVOLUTION BEFORE.

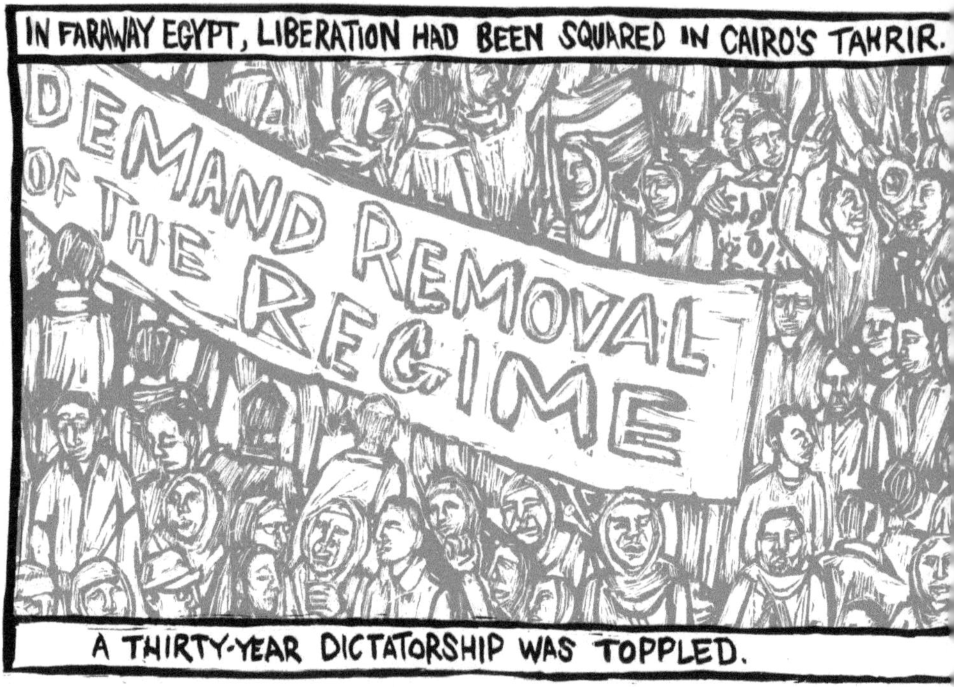
IN FARAWAY EGYPT, LIBERATION HAD BEEN SQUARED IN CAIRO'S TAHRIR.
DEMAND REMOVAL OF THE REGIME
A THIRTY-YEAR DICTATORSHIP WAS TOPPLED.

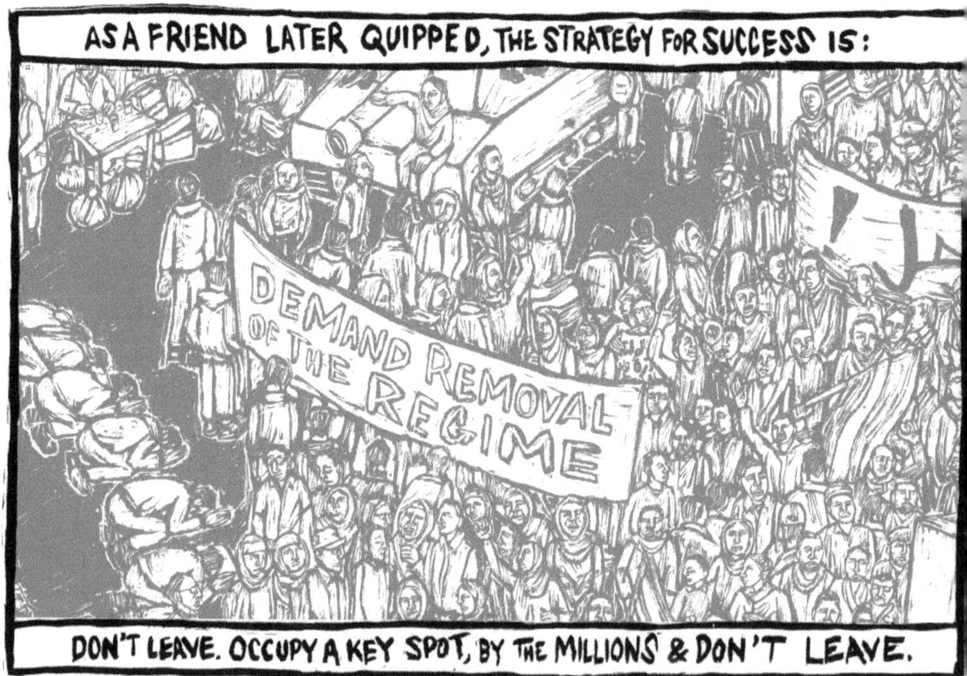
AS A FRIEND LATER QUIPPED, THE STRATEGY FOR SUCCESS IS:
DEMAND REMOVAL OF THE REGIME
DON'T LEAVE. OCCUPY A KEY SPOT, BY THE MILLIONS & DON'T LEAVE.

YET THE VICTORY WAS NOT SIMPLY DUE TO SHEER NUMBERS.

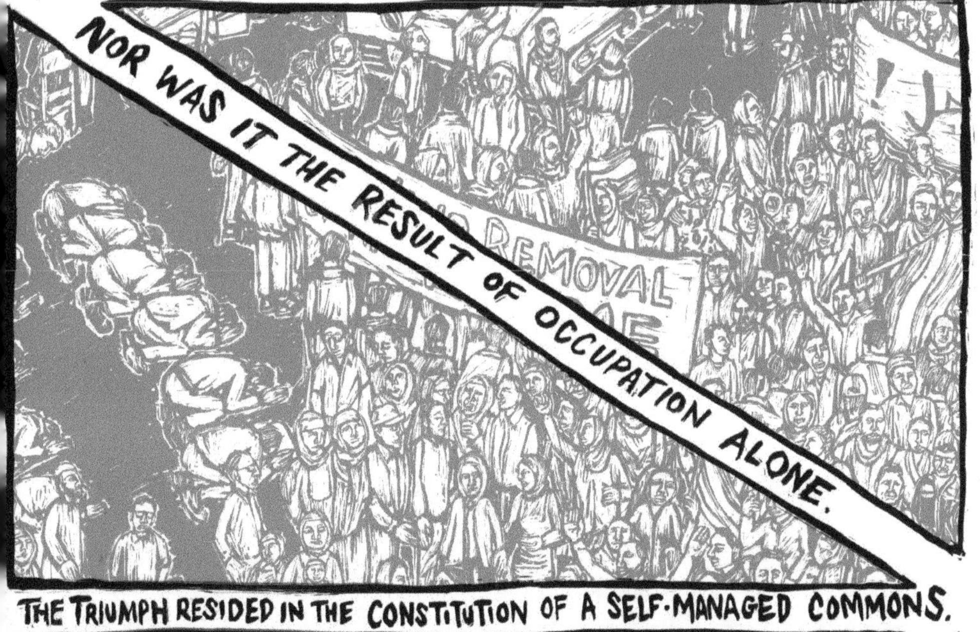
NOR WAS IT THE RESULT OF OCCUPATION ALONE.
REMOVAL

THE TRIUMPH RESIDED IN THE CONSTITUTION OF A SELF-MANAGED COMMONS.

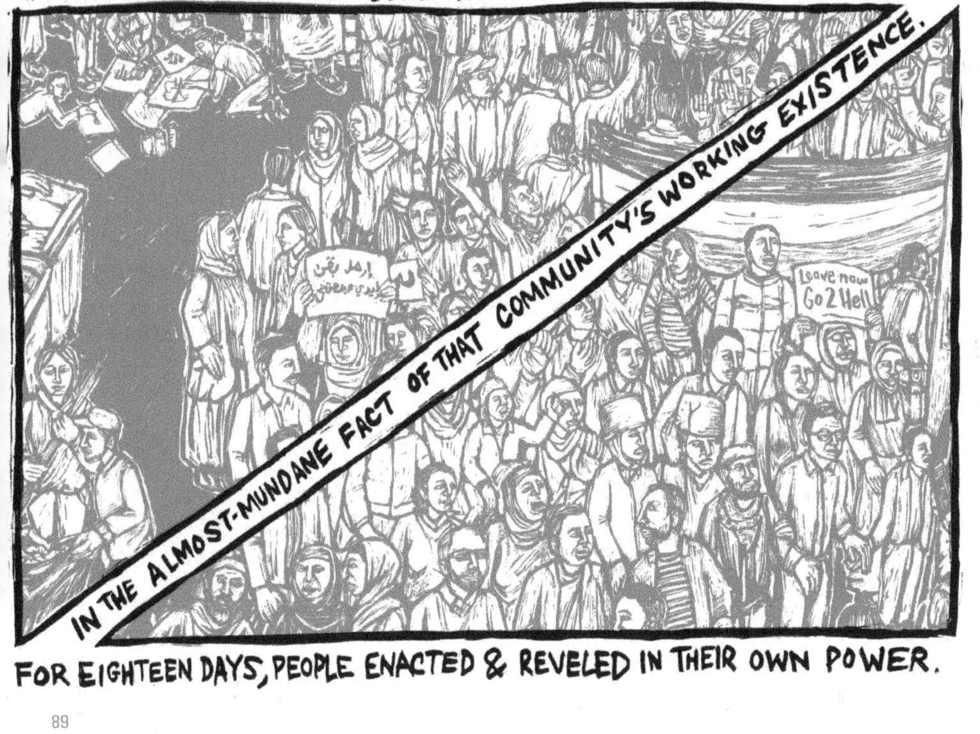
IN THE ALMOST-MUNDANE FACT OF THAT COMMUNITY'S WORKING EXISTENCE.
Leave now Go 2 Hell

FOR EIGHTEEN DAYS, PEOPLE ENACTED & REVELED IN THEIR OWN POWER.

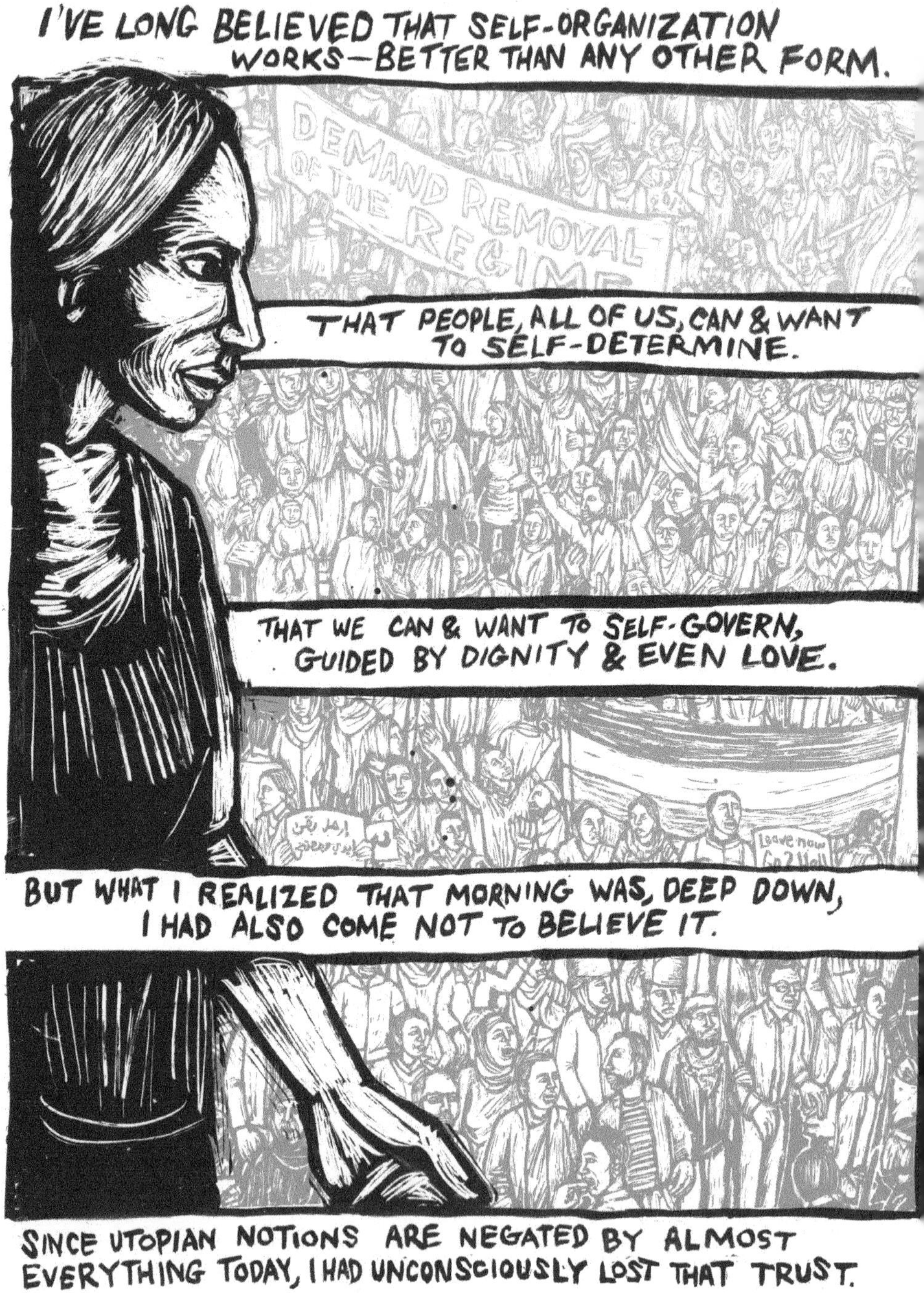
I'VE LONG BELIEVED THAT SELF-ORGANIZATION WORKS—BETTER THAN ANY OTHER FORM.
DEMAND REMOVAL OF THE REGIME
THAT PEOPLE, ALL OF US, CAN & WANT TO SELF-DETERMINE.
THAT WE CAN & WANT TO SELF-GOVERN, GUIDED BY DIGNITY & EVEN LOVE.
Leave now
BUT WHAT I REALIZED THAT MORNING WAS, DEEP DOWN, I HAD ALSO COME NOT TO BELIEVE IT.
SINCE UTOPIAN NOTIONS ARE NEGATED BY ALMOST EVERYTHING TODAY, I HAD UNCONSCIOUSLY LOST THAT TRUST.

THE UPRISING BEGAN WITH A SURPRISE, AS IF FROM NOWHERE. OVERNIGHT, PEOPLE DISCOVERED THEIR COLLECTIVE STRENGTH.

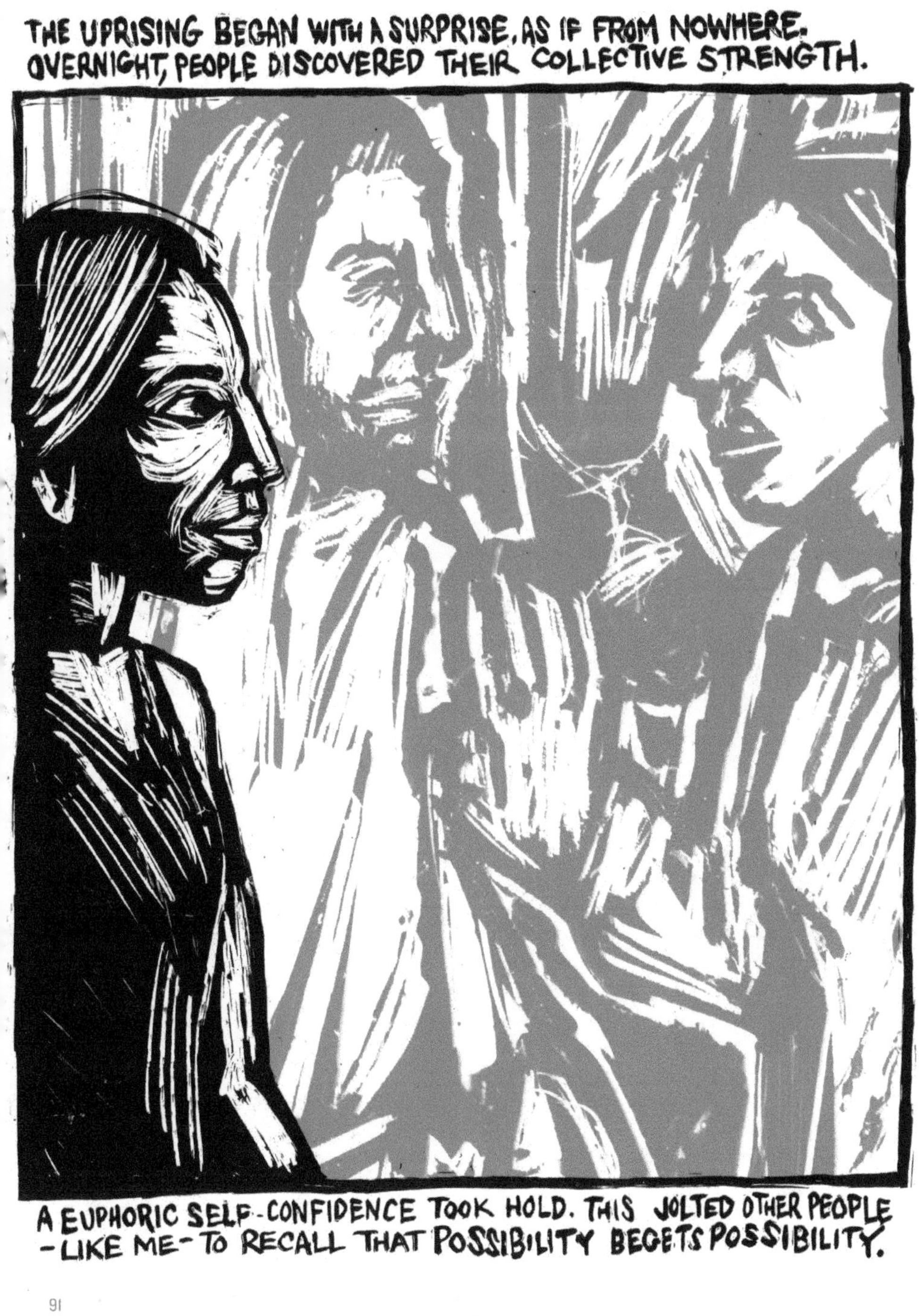

A EUPHORIC SELF-CONFIDENCE TOOK HOLD. THIS JOLTED OTHER PEOPLE -LIKE ME- TO RECALL THAT POSSIBILITY BEGETS POSSIBILITY.

THOSE OF US WHO ARE HERETICS ARE ALSO ARCHAEOLOGISTS. WE SIFT THROUGH THE SHARDS OF PAST EXPERIMENTS, BURIED IN THE RICH SUBTERRANEAN, FOR EVIDENCE OF WHAT HANNAH ARENDT CALLED "THE LOST TREASURE" OF REVOLUTIONS, THE "ORGANIZATIONAL IMPULSES OF THE PEOPLE THEMSELVES":

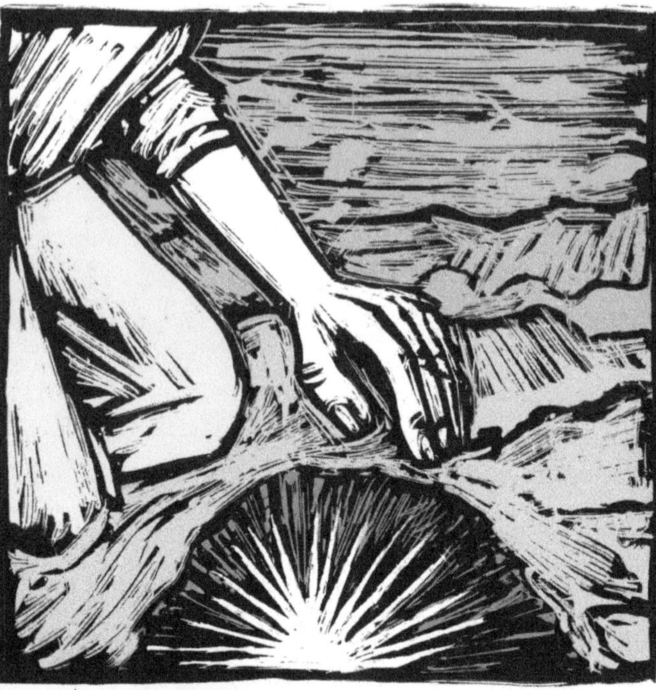

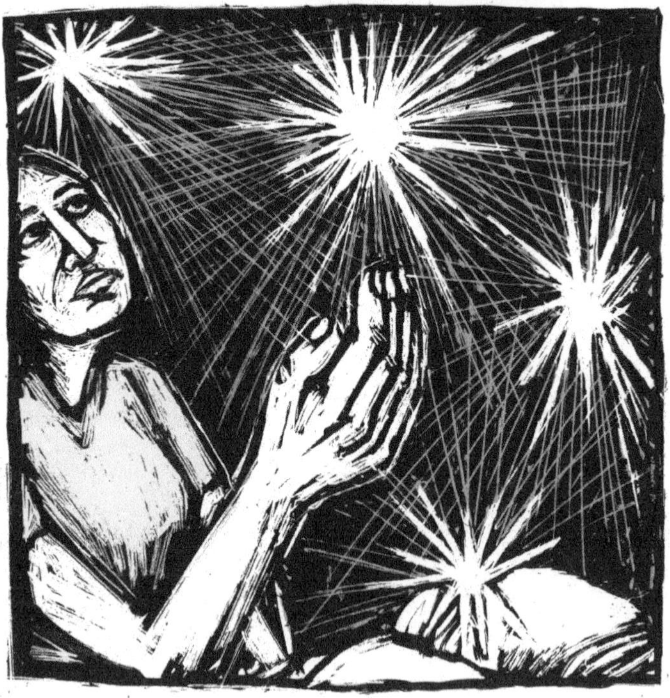

COUNCILS, MILITIAS, CONFEDERATIONS, SOVIETS, CONSULTAS, ASSEMBLIES...

THE INFINITE LIVED INNOVATIONS IN BOTTOM-UP SOCIAL RELATIONS.

WE STRING THESE GEMS TOGETHER, TOSSING THEM IN THE AIR, AS NEW CELESTIAL BODIES TO GUIDE OTHERS.

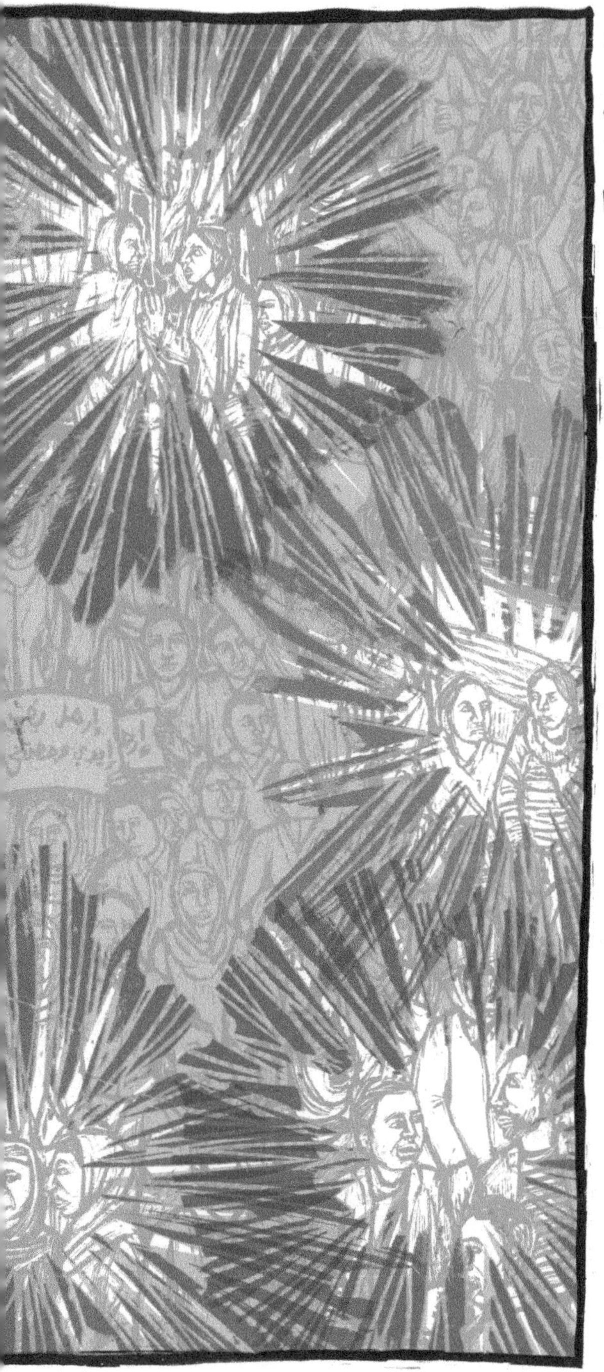

IN CAIRO, FROM THESE GLITTERING SCRAPS, PEOPLE BUILT THEIR OWN CITY IN A SQUARE, RAPIDLY, WITHOUT LEADERS.

AN IMPROMPTU PRISM, AFFORDING PARTIAL ANSWERS TO THE LOWLIEST & LOFTIEST OF QUESTIONS:

"IN THE ABSENCE OF COERCION, WHO WILL TAKE OUT THE TRASH?"

"HOW CAN WE TRANSFORM GENDER RELATIONS?"

THAT MORNING, WHEN MUBARAK FELL, MY MIND WAS FLOODED WITH IMAGES, GLEANED FROM THE EYEWITNESS ACCOUNTS I'D HUNGRILY READ, OF *HOW* PEOPLE CRAFTED THEIR AUTONOMOUS SOCIETY, OUT OF NECESSITY & UNDER SOMETIMES-DEADLY ADVERSITY.

OF HOW PEOPLE PROTECTED EACH OTHER:

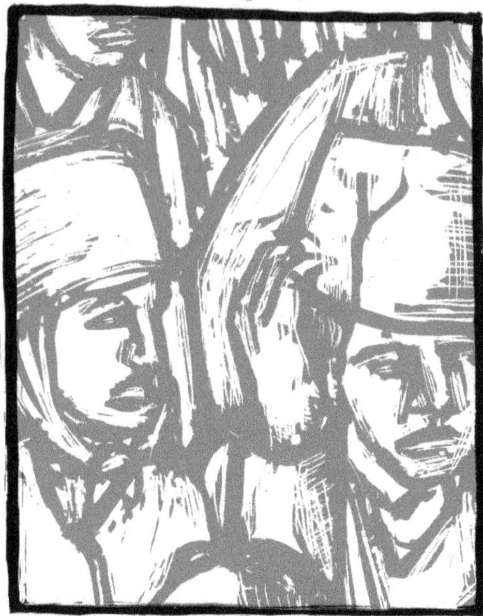

THE MAKESHIFT HELMETS, FROM BUCKETS & BOTTLES, SAUCEPANS & FOAM.

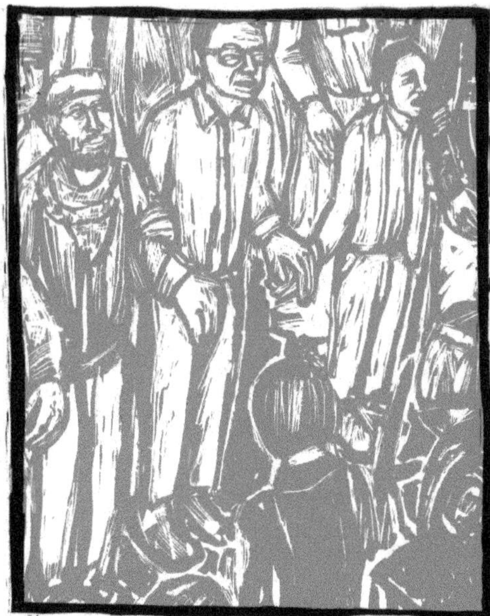

THE SELF-DEFENSE COMMITTEES & THEIR TEMPORARY BARRICADES & CHECKPOINTS

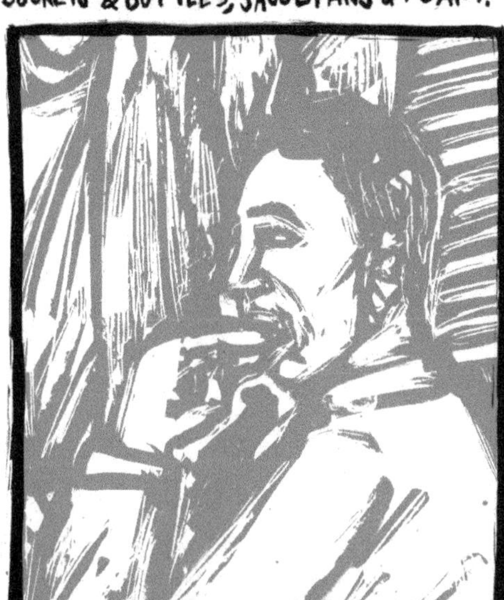

WHISTLING AS A SIGNAL WHEN ASSISTANCE WAS NEEDED,

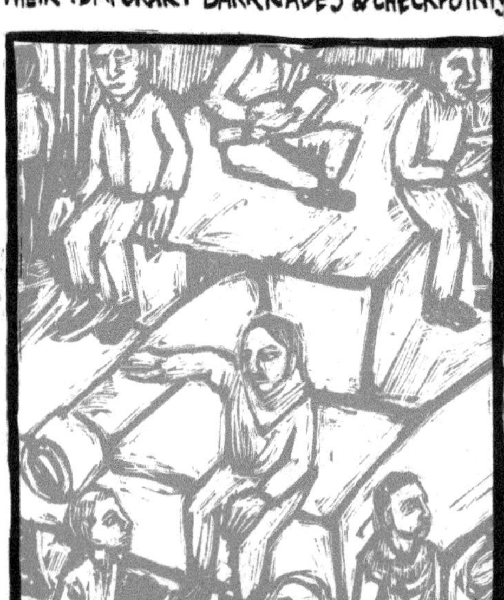

OR PEOPLE SLEEPING & SITTING ON TANKS, TO NEUTRALIZE THEM AS WEAPONS.

OF HOW PEOPLE CARED FOR EACH OTHER:

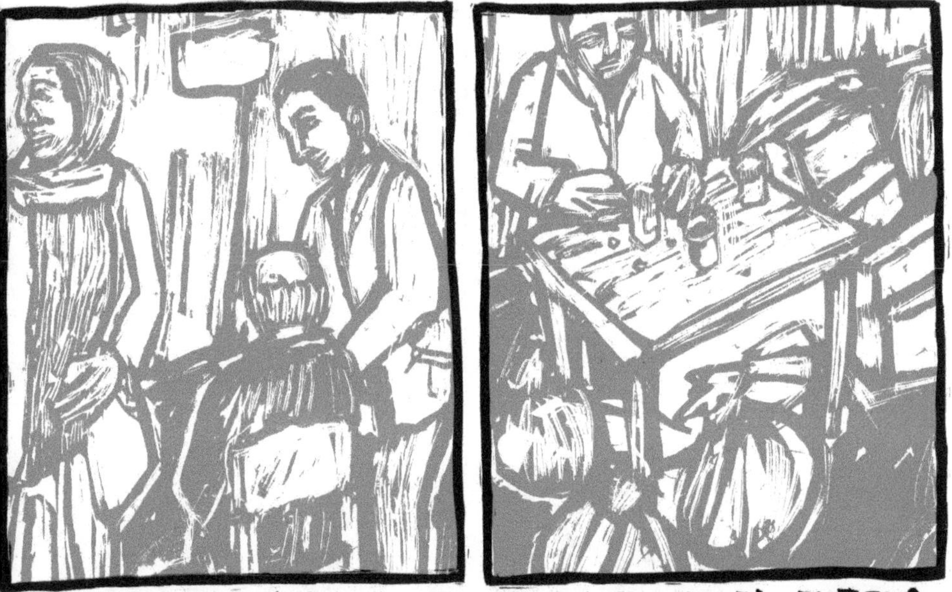

THE CLINICS & PHARMACIES, IN ALLEYWAYS & A NOW-FORMER FAST-FOOD SPOT, WHERE VOLUNTEER DOCTORS IN WHITE COATS FREELY DISPENSED MEDICAL AID.

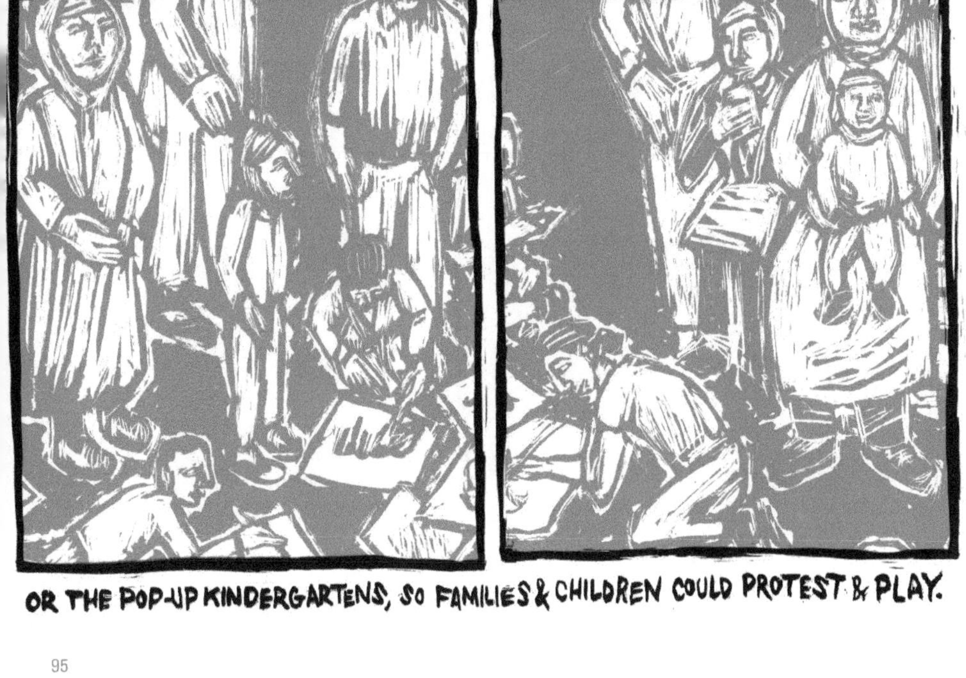

OR THE POP-UP KINDERGARTENS, SO FAMILIES & CHILDREN COULD PROTEST & PLAY.

OF HOW PEOPLE PROVIDED FOR EACH OTHER:

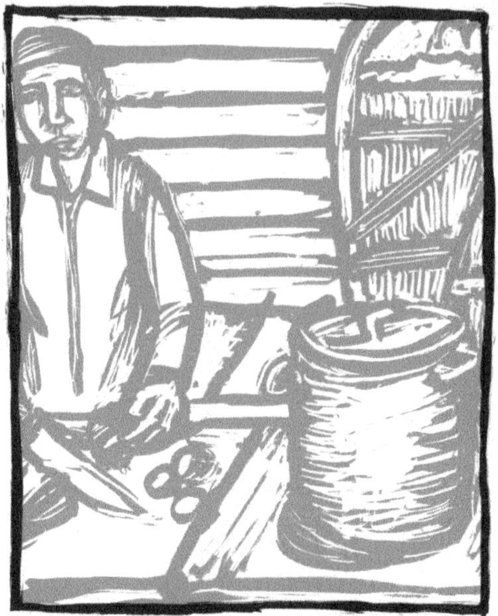

THE COMMUNAL KITCHENS THAT ALSO SERVED AS SKILL SHARES,

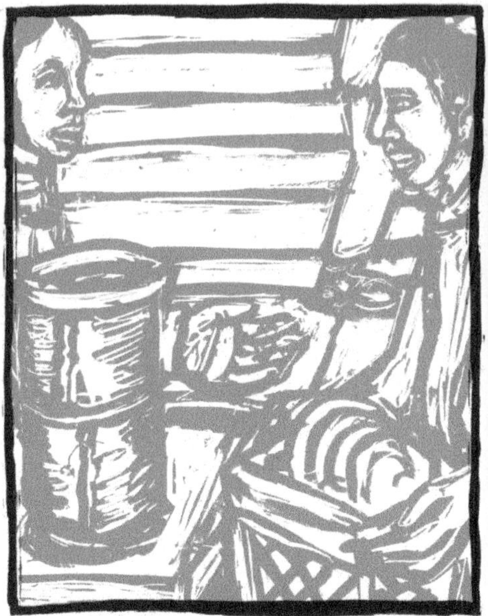

IN WHICH EACH VOLUNTEER WOULD SHOW THE NEXT PERSON WHAT TO DO BEFORE LEAVING

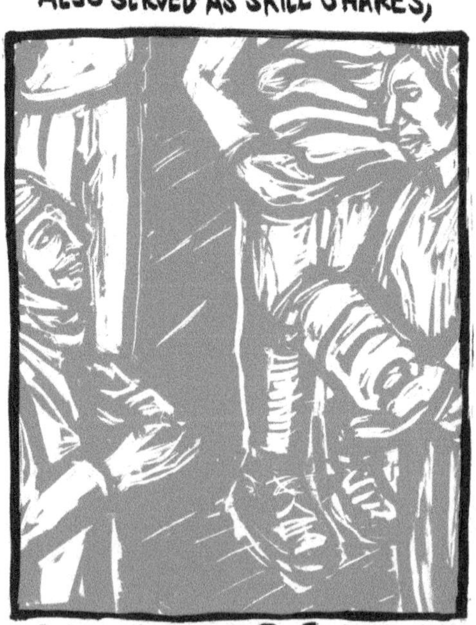

THE DAILY ARRIVAL OF TENTS & BLANKETS & NEWSPAPERS PUBLICLY POSTED.

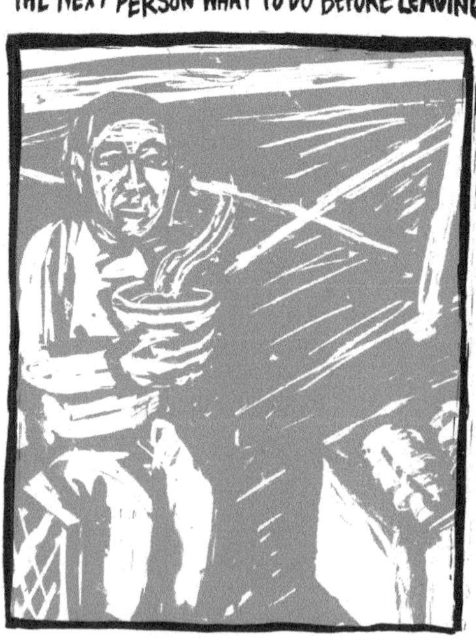

ALMOST EVERYTHING FOR EVERYONE, FREE.

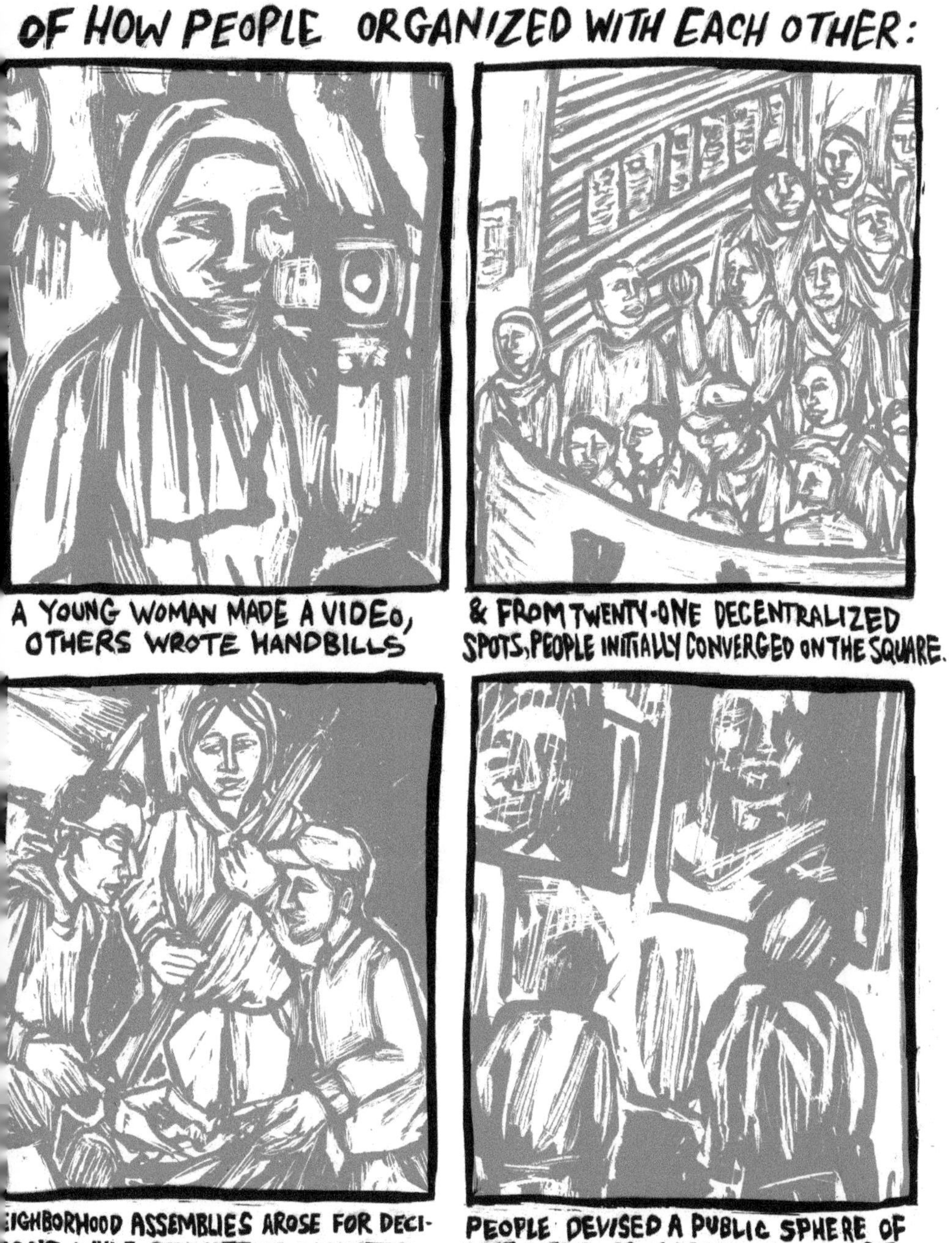
OF HOW PEOPLE ORGANIZED WITH EACH OTHER:
A YOUNG WOMAN MADE A VIDEO, OTHERS WROTE HANDBILLS
& FROM TWENTY-ONE DECENTRALIZED SPOTS, PEOPLE INITIALLY CONVERGED ON THE SQUARE.
EIGHBORHOOD ASSEMBLIES AROSE FOR DECI-IONS, WHILE COMMITTEES INVENTED STEMS FOR GARBAGE COLLECTION, RE-YCLING & CLEANUP.
PEOPLE DEVISED A PUBLIC SPHERE OF INDIE MEDIA, SPEAKERS' AREAS & ART, & MARTYRS' WALLS TO REMEMBER THOSE KILLED IN THIS BATTLE.

THE AFTERNOON OF THE MORNING WHEN MUBARAK WAS DEPOSED, I WENT TO A SOLIDARITY CELEBRATION IN SAN FRANCISCO.

"CAN YOU BELIEVE IT?" SAID AN EGYPTIAN EMIGRANT, FRESH FROM ANOTHER CELEBRATION AT HIS MOSQUE.

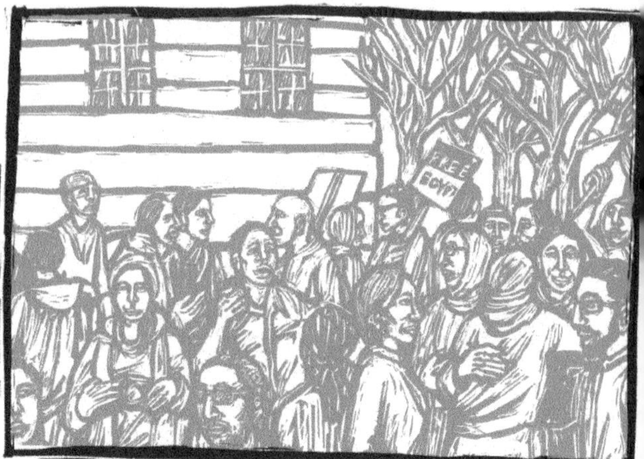
FREE EGYPT

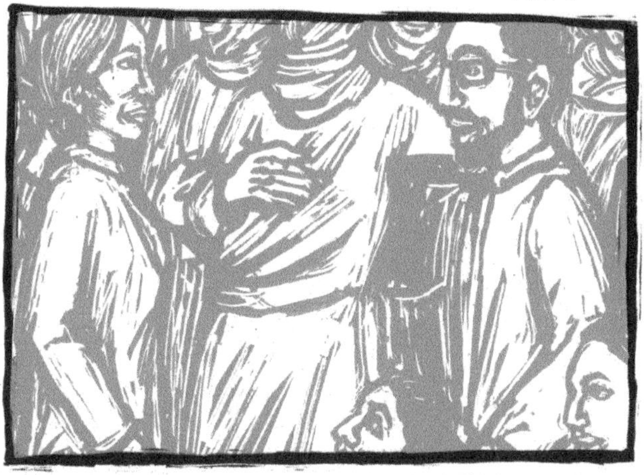

WE'D NEVER MET.

HE INTRODUCED ME TO HIS FAMILY HERE, EXPLAINED THAT HE'D BEEN IN CONSTANT TOUCH WITH RELATIVES IN TAHRIR & FOR AN HOUR, TOLD ME ABOUT ALL THAT HAD CHANGED.

"MY PEOPLE DID IT THEMSELVES, SHARING ALL."

"MUSLIMS & CHRISTIANS WERE UNITED."

"WOMEN WERE EQUAL PARTICIPANTS & SEXUAL HARASSMENT SEEMED TO DISAPPEAR."

HIS FOUR DAUGHTERS, ALL UNDER TEN YEARS OLD, SMILED UP AT ME.

"IT WAS NEVER LIKE THAT BEFORE."

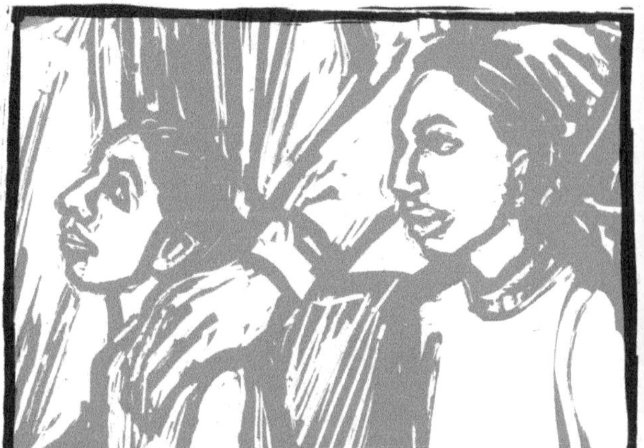

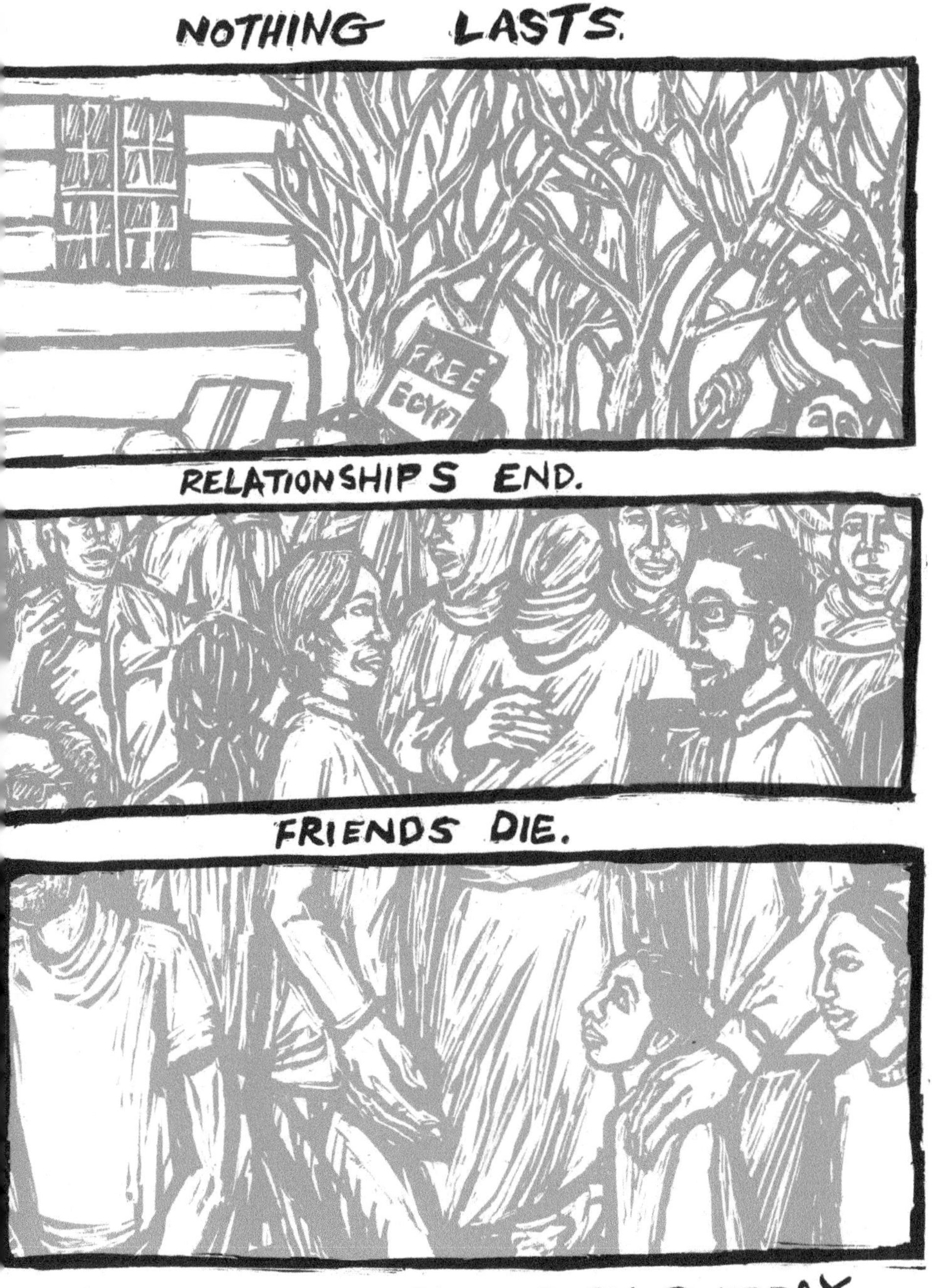
NOTHING LASTS.
FREE EGYPT
RELATIONSHIPS END.
FRIENDS DIE.
EVEN CAPITALISM WILL BE HISTORY SOMEDAY.

IT'S WHAT WE DO TO REAWAKEN EACH OTHER THAT MATTERS, BREATHING LIFE INTO SELF-ORGANIZATION, THE WORKING ACTUALITY OF FREEDOM.

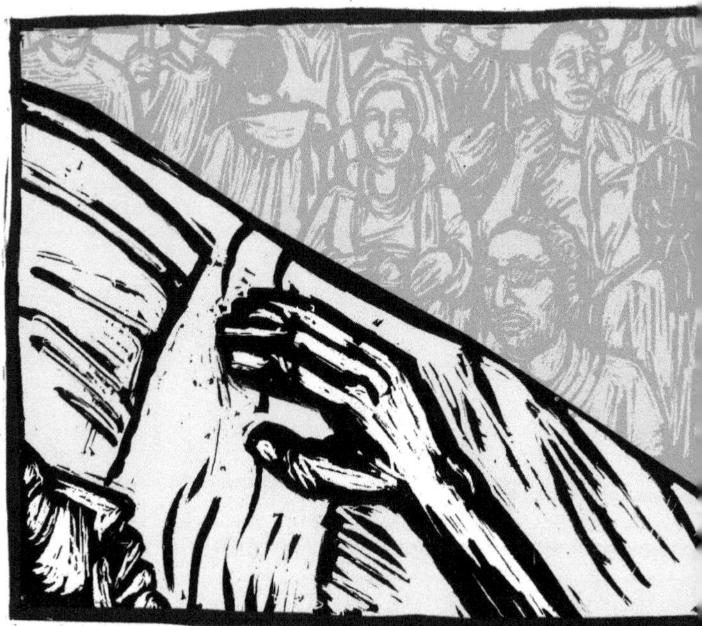

THAT'S THE VICTORY, THE REVOLUTION, THE TRUTH OF OUR POWER:

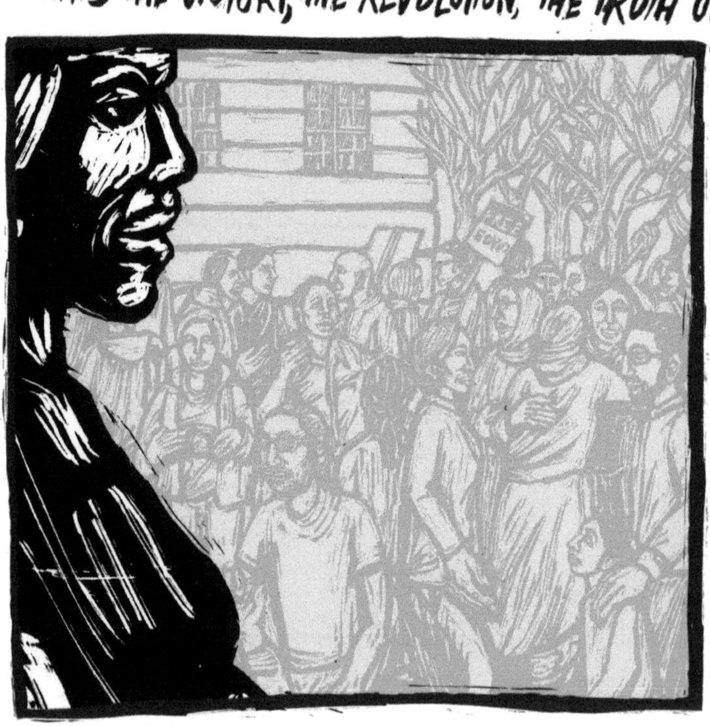

THAT WE KNOW HOW TO CREATE LIVES WORTH LIVING, KNOWING THAT SUCH MOMENTS, TOO, WON'T LAST.

YET AFTERWARD, WHEN THE SQUARES & CAPITOLS ARE FORCIBLY EMPTIED, THE WORLD NEVER FULLY GOES BACK TO NORMAL.

WE AREN'T THE SAME PEOPLE.

SOME OF OUR EXPERIMENTATION STICKS, MAKING US A LITTLE LESS ESTRANGED, A LITTLE MORE HEARTENED.

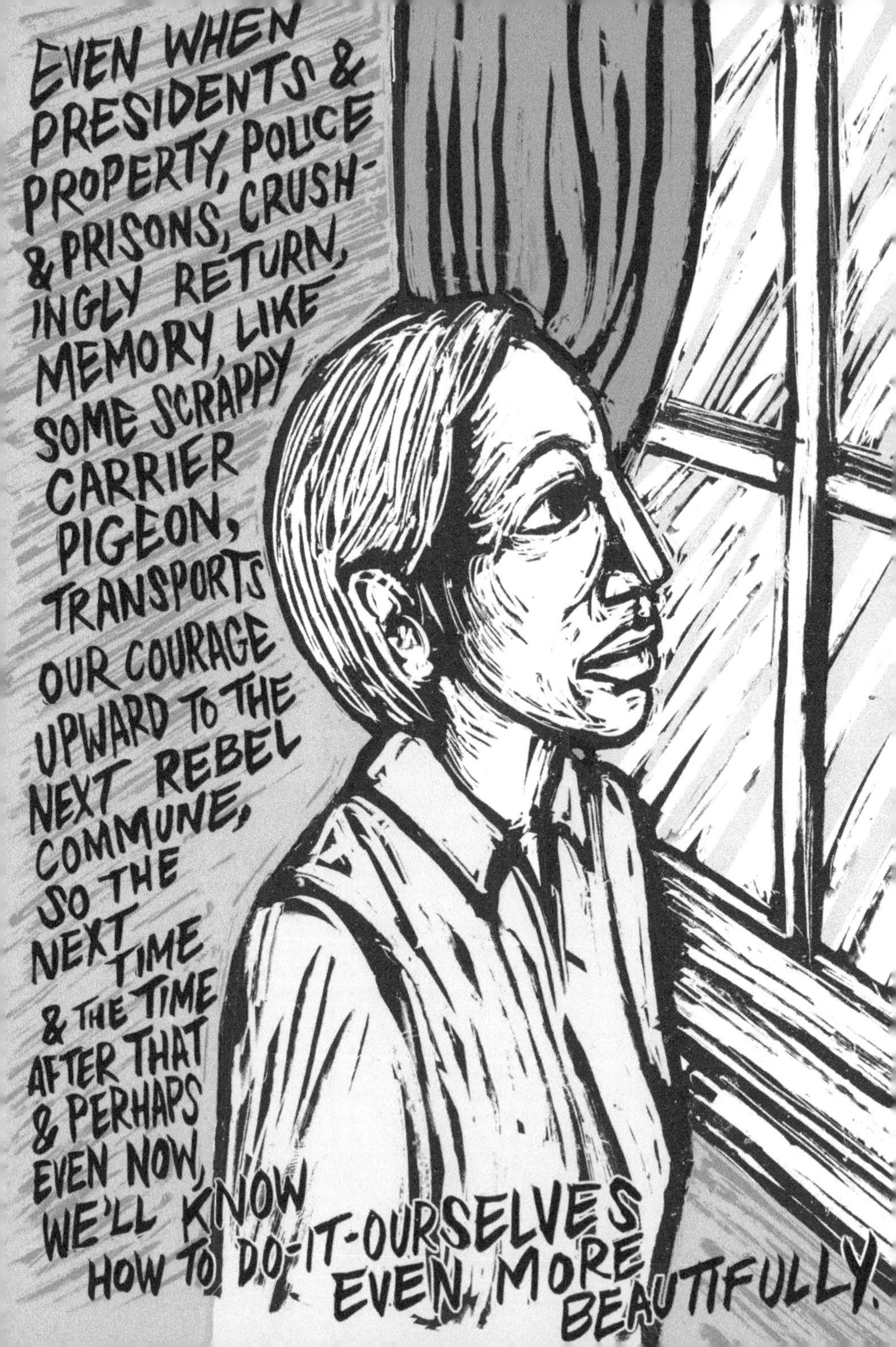
EVEN WHEN
PRESIDENTS &
PROPERTY, POLICE
& PRISONS, CRUSH-
INGLY RETURN,
MEMORY, LIKE
SOME SCRAPPY
CARRIER
PIGEON,
TRANSPORTS
OUR COURAGE
UPWARD TO THE
NEXT REBEL
COMMUNE,
SO THE
NEXT TIME
& THE TIME
AFTER THAT
& PERHAPS
EVEN NOW,
WE'LL KNOW
HOW TO DO-IT-OURSELVES
EVEN MORE
BEAUTIFULLY.

ABOUT THE CONTRIBUTORS

Cindy Milstein is the author of *Anarchism and Its Aspirations* (AK Press, 2010), and has contributed to anthologies such as *Realizing the Impossible: Art against Authority* (AK Press, 2007). She is an Institute for Anarchist Studies collective member, was actively engaged in Occupy Philly for months, and has been involved in collective projects ranging from Black Sheep Books to the Don't Just (Not) Vote campaign, from the New World from Below convergence to the Renewing the Anarchist Tradition conference.

Erik Ruin is a printmaker, shadow-puppeteer, and occasional maker/editor of various publications, including the anthology *Realizing the Impossible: Art against Authority* (coedited with Josh MacPhee, AK Press, 2007). He frequently works collaboratively with other artists or activist campaigns, such as in imagery created for urban farming and prison abolition groups, and collectively, most prominently as a founding member of the Justseeds Artists' Cooperative.

Josh MacPhee is a designer, artist, activist, and archivist. He is a member of both the Justseeds Artists' Cooperative and Occuprint collective. His most recent books are *Celebrate People's History! The Poster Book of Resistance and Revolution* (Feminist Press, 2010) and *Signs of Change: Social Movement Cultures 1960s to Now* (coedited with Dara Greenwald, AK Press, 2010). He recently helped open the Interference Archive, a public collection of cultural materials produced by social movements.

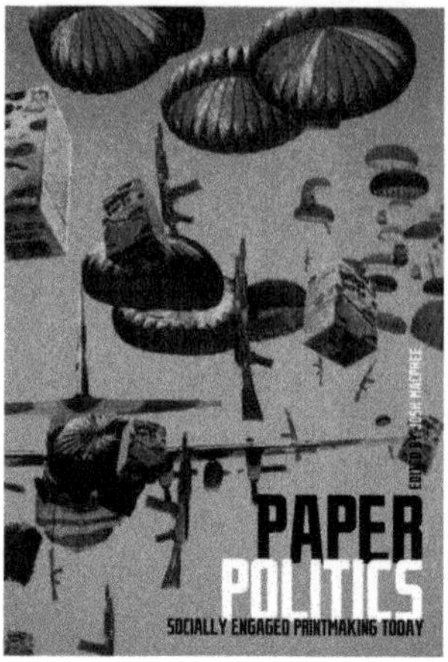
PAPER
POLITICS
SOCIALLY ENGAGED PRINTMAKING TODAY

Paper Politics: Socially Engaged Printmaking Today
Edited by Josh MacPhee
ISBN: 978-1-60486-090-0
$24.95 160 full color pages

Paper Politics: Socially Engaged Printmaking Today is a major collection of contemporary politically and socially engaged printmaking. This full-color book showcases print art that uses themes of social justice and global equity to engage community members in political conversation. Based on an art exhibition that has traveled to a dozen cities in North America, *Paper Politics* features artwork by over 200 international artists; an eclectic collection of work by both activist and non-activist printmakers who have felt the need to respond to the monumental trends and events of our times.

Paper Politics presents a breathtaking tour of the many modalities of printing by hand: relief, intaglio, lithography, serigraph, collagraph, monotype, and photography. In addition to these techniques, included are more traditional media used to convey political thought, finely crafted stencils and silk-screens intended for wheat pasting in the street. Artists range from the well established (Sue Coe, Swoon, Carlos Cortez) to the up-and-coming (Favianna Rodriguez, Chris Stain, Nicole Schulman), from street artists (BORF, You Are Beautiful) to rock poster makers (EMEK, Bughouse).

Praise:
"Let's face it, most collections of activist art suck. Either esthetic concerns are front and center and the politics that motivate such creation are pushed to the margin, or politics prevail and artistic quality is an afterthought. With the heart of an activist and the eye of an artist, Josh MacPhee miraculously manages to do justice to both. *Paper Politics* is singularly impressive." —Stephen Duncombe, author of *Dream: Re-imagining Progressive Politics in an Age of Fantasy*

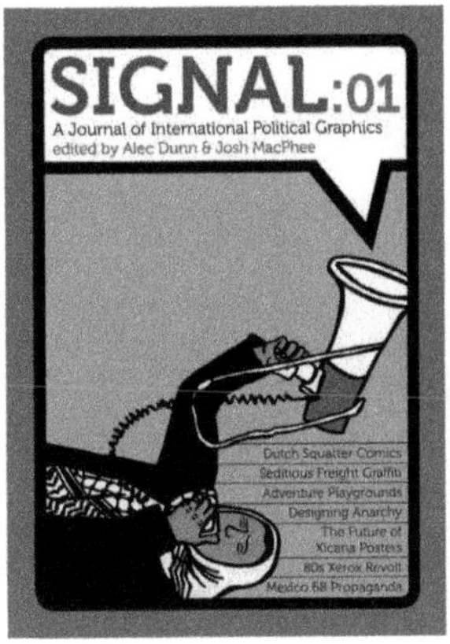
SIGNAL:01
A Journal of International Political Graphics
edited by Alec Dunn & Josh MacPhee
Dutch Squatter Comics
Seditious Freight Graffiti
Adventure Playgrounds
Designing Anarchy
The Future of Xicana Posters
80s Xerox Revolt
Mexico 68 Propaganda

Signal:01
Edited by Alec Dunn & Josh MacPhee
ISBN: 978-1-60486-091-7
$14.95   148 full color pages

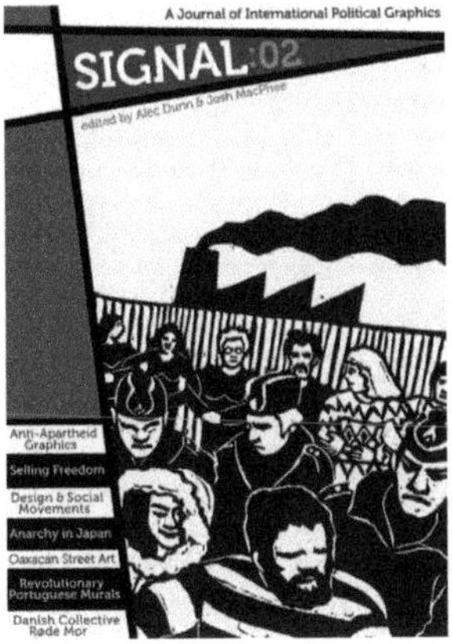
A Journal of International Political Graphics
SIGNAL:02
edited by Alec Dunn & Josh MacPhee
Anti-Apartheid Graphics
Selling Freedom
Design & Social Movements
Anarchy in Japan
Oaxacan Street Art
Revolutionary Portuguese Murals
Danish Collective Røde Mor

Signal:02
Edited by Alec Dunn & Josh MacPhee
ISBN: 978-1-60486-298-0
$14.95   160 full color pages

Signal is an ongoing book series dedicated to documenting and sharing compelling graphics, art projects, and cultural movements of international resistance and liberation struggles. Artists and cultural workers have been at the center of upheavals and revolts the world over, from the painters and poets in the Paris Commune to the poster makers and street theatre performers of the recent Occupy movement. *Signal* will bring these artists and their work to a new audience, digging deep through our common history to unearth their images and stories. We have no doubt that *Signal* will come to serve as a unique and irreplaceable resource for activist artists and academic researchers, as well as an active forum for critique of the role of art in revolution.

In the U.S. there is a tendency to focus only on the artworks produced within our shores or from English speaking producers. *Signal* reaches beyond those bounds, bringing material produced the world over, translated from dozens of languages and collected from both the present and decades past. Though it is a full-color printed publication, *Signal* is not limited to the graphic arts. Within its pages you will find political posters and fine arts, comics and murals, street art, site-specific works, zines, art collectives, documentation of performance and articles on the often overlooked but essential role all of these have played in struggles around the world.

Praise:
"*Signal* reads like a magazine in that it consists of a number of smaller, independent articles but the loose continuity of subject holds it together as a book. As a series, this is going to be a great resource. Dunn and MacPhee are filling a void in terms of political graphics; there's a lot of material for them to cover and this is solid start." —Printeresting.org

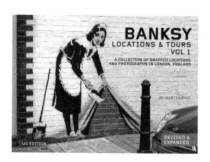

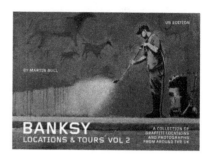

BANKSY
LOCATIONS & TOURS
VOL 1
A COLLECTION OF GRAFFITI LOCATIONS AND PHOTOGRAPHS IN LONDON, ENGLAND
BY MARTIN BULL
US EDITION
REVISED & EXPANDED

Banksy Location and Tours Volume I: A Collection of Graffiti Locations and Photographs in London, England
Photographer and Editor: Martin Bull
ISBN: 978-1-60486-320-8
$20 176 full color pages

US EDITION
BY MARTIN BULL
BANKSY
LOCATIONS & TOURS VOL 2
A COLLECTION OF GRAFFITI LOCATIONS AND PHOTOGRAPHS FROM AROUND THE UK

Banksy Location and Tours Volume 2: A Collection of Graffiti Locations and Photographs from around the UK
Photographer and Editor: Martin Bull
ISBN: 978-1-60486-330-7
$20 180 full color pages

When it comes to art, London is best known for its galleries, not its graffiti. However, not if photographer Martin Bull has anything to say about it. While newspapers and magazines the world over send their critics to review the latest Damien Hirst show at the Tate Modern, Bull, in turn, is out taking photos of the latest street installations by guerilla art icon Banksy.

In *Volume I*'s three guided tours, Martin Bull documents sixty-five London sites where one can see some of the most important works by the legendary political artist. Boasting over 100 color photos, *Banksy Locations and Tours Volume I* also includes graffiti by many of Banksy's peers, including Eine, Faile, El Chivo, Arofish, Cept, Space Invader, Blek Le Rat, D*face, and Shepherd Fairey.

Volume 2 rounds up the rest of Banksy's UK graffiti from the last five years. It includes over 100 different locations and 200 color photographs of Banksy's street art; information, random facts, and idle chit-chat on each location; a full walking tour of his remaining work in Bristol, England; and snippets of graffiti by several other artists.

Praise:
"Martin Bull charts the mysterious appearances—and sadly, sloppy destruction—of Banksy graffiti all over London, complete with maps and notes on the present condition of his works. Bull's unpretentious style and dedication to graffiti art comes across in everything he writes."
—London Sketchbook on *Volume I*

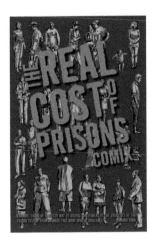

THE REAL COST OF PRISONS
COMIX

The Real Cost Of Prisons Comix
Edited by Lois Ahrens; Illustrated by Kevin Pyle, Sabrina Jones, and Susan Willmarth
ISBN: 978-1-60486-034-4
$14.95   104 pages

One out of every hundred adults in the U.S. is in prison. This book provides a crash course in what drives mass incarceration, the human and community costs, and how to stop the numbers from going even higher. This volume collects the three comic books published by the Real Cost of Prisons Project. The stories and statistical information in each comic book is thoroughly researched and documented.

Prison Town: Paying the Price tells the story of how the financing and site locations of prisons affects the people of rural communities in which prison are built. It also tells the story of how mass incarceration affects people of urban communities where the majority of incarcerated people come from.

Prisoners of the War on Drugs includes the history of the war on drugs, mandatory minimums, how racism creates harsher sentences for people of color, stories on how the war on drugs works against women, three strikes laws, obstacles to coming home after incarceration, and how mass incarceration destabilizes neighborhoods.

Prisoners of a Hard Life: Women and Their Children includes stories about women trapped by mandatory sentencing and the "costs" of incarceration for women and their families. Also included are alternatives to the present system, a glossary, and footnotes.

Praise:
"I cannot think of a better way to arouse the public to the cruelties of the prison system than to make this book widely available." —Howard Zinn

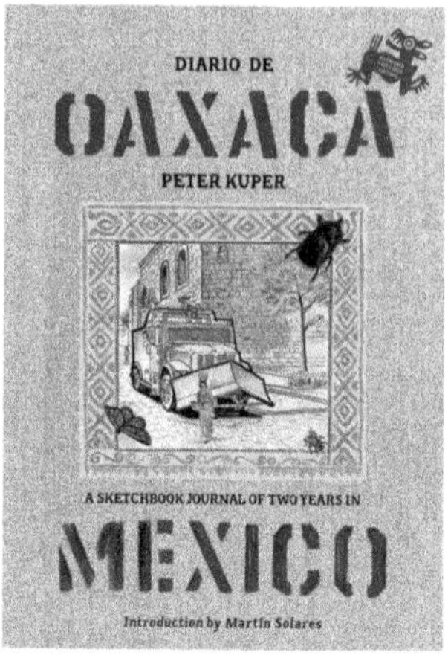
DIARIO DE
OAXACA
PETER KUPER
A SKETCHBOOK JOURNAL OF TWO YEARS IN
MEXICO
Introduction by Martín Solares

Diario De Oaxaca: A Sketchbook Journal of Two Years in Mexico
Peter Kuper, with an Introduction by Martín Solares
ISBN: 978-1-62963-441-8
$24.95 240 full color pages

Painting a vivid, personal portrait of social and political upheaval in Oaxaca, Mexico, this unique memoir employs comics, bilingual essays, photos, and sketches to chronicle the events that unfolded around a teachers' strike and led to a seven-month siege.

When award-winning cartoonist Peter Kuper and his wife and daughter moved to the beautiful 16th-century colonial town of Oaxaca in 2006, they planned to spend a quiet year or two enjoying a different culture and taking a break from the U.S. political climate under the Bush administration. What they hadn't counted on was landing in the epicenter of Mexico's biggest political struggle in recent years. Timely and compelling, this extraordinary firsthand account presents a distinct artistic vision of Oaxacan life, from explorations of the beauty of the environment to graphic portrayals of the fight between strikers and government troops that left more than twenty people dead, including American journalist Brad Will.

This expanded paperback edition includes 32 pages of new material.

Praise:
"Kuper is a colossus; I have been in awe of him for over 20 years. Teachers and students everywhere take heart: Kuper has in these pages born witness to our seemingly endless struggle to educate and to be educated in the face of institutions that really don't give a damn. In this ruined age we need Kuper's unsparing compassionate visionary artistry like we need hope."
—Junot Díaz, Pulitzer Prize winning author of *The Brief Wondrous Life of Oscar Wao*

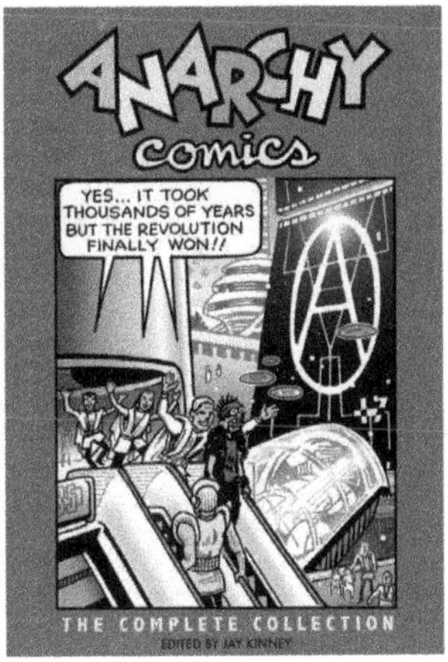
ANARCHY
comics
YES... IT TOOK THOUSANDS OF YEARS BUT THE REVOLUTION FINALLY WON!!
THE COMPLETE COLLECTION
EDITED BY JAY KINNEY

Anarchy Comics: The Complete Collection
Edited by Jay Kinney
ISBN: 978-1-60486-531-8
$20.00 224 pages

Anarchy Comics: The Complete Collection brings together the legendary four issues of *Anarchy Comics* (1978-1986), the underground comic that melded anarchist politics with a punk sensibility, producing a riveting mix of satire, revolt, and artistic experimentation. This international anthology collects the comic stories of all thirty contributors from the U.S., Great Britain, France, Germany, Netherlands, Spain, and Canada.

In addition to the complete issues of *Anarchy Comics*, the anthology features previously unpublished work by Jay Kinney and Sharon Rudahl, along with a detailed introduction by Kinney, which traces the history of the comic he founded and provides entertaining anecdotes about the process of herding an international crowd of anarchistic cats.

Contributors include: Jay Kinney, Yves Frémion, Gerhard Seyfried, Sharon Rudahl, Steve Stiles, Donald Rooum, Paul Mavrides, Adam Cornford, Spain Rodriguez, Melinda Gebbie, Gilbert Shelton, Volny, John Burnham, Cliff Harper, Ruby Ray, Peter Pontiac, Marcel Trublin, Albo Helm, Steve Lafler, Gary Panter, Greg Irons, Dave Lester, Marion Lydebrooke, Matt Feazell, Pepe Moreno, Norman Dog, Zorca, R. Diggs (Harry Driggs), Harry Robins, and Byron Werner.

Praise:
"*Anarchy Comics* was an education I never got in school. I learned more deep truths about the way human megatribes operate (while at the same time being greatly amused by the superb art and writing) than from any textbook. Decades later, the insights I gleaned from these brilliant comics still affect the way I view global events."
—Mark Frauenfelder, founder of boingboing.net

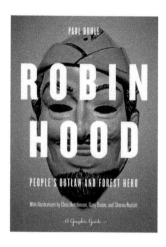

PAUL BUHLE
ROBIN HOOD
PEOPLE'S OUTLAW AND FOREST HERO
With Illustrations by Chris Hutchinson, Gary Dumm, and Sharon Rudahl
A Graphic Guide

Robin Hood: People's Outlaw and Forest Hero, A Graphic Guide
Paul Buhle with Chris Hutchinson, Gary Dumm, and Sharon Rudahl
ISBN: 978-1-60486-318-5
$15.00 112 pages

Where and what was Robin Hood? Why is an outlaw from fourteenth century England still a hero today, with films, festivals and songs dedicated to his living memory?

This book explores the mysteries, the historical evidence, and the trajectory that led to centuries of village festivals around Mayday and the green space of nature unconquered by the forces in power. Great revolutionaries including William Morris adopted Robin as hero, children's books offered many versions, and Robin entered modern popular culture with cheap novels, silent films and comics.

There, in the world of popular culture, Robin Hood continues to holds unique and secure place. The "bad-good" hero of pulp urban fiction of the 1840s-50s, and more important, the Western outlaw who thwarts the bankers in pulps, films, and comics, is essentially Robin Hood. So are Zorro, the Cisco Kid, and countless Robin Hood knockoff characters in various media.

Robin Hood has a special resonance for leftwing influences on American popular culture in Hollywood, film and television. During the 1930s-50s, future blacklist victims devised radical plots of "people's outlaws," including anti-fascist guerilla fighters, climaxing in *The Adventures of Robin Hood*, network television 1955-58, written under cover by victims of the Blacklist, seen by more viewers than any other version of Robin Hood.

Robin Hood: People's Outlaw and Forest Hero also features 30 pages of collages and comic art, recuperating the artistic interpretations of Robin from seven centuries, and offering new comic art as a comic-within-a book.

The Housing Monster

prole.info

The Housing Monster
Prole.info
ISBN: 978-1-60486-530-1
$14.95   160 Pages

The Housing Monster is a scathing illustrated essay that takes one seemingly simple, every-day thing—a house—and looks at the social relations that surround it. Moving from intensely personal thoughts and interactions to large-scale political and economic forces, it reads alter-nately like a worker's diary, a short story, a psychology of everyday life, a historical account, an introduction to Marxist critique of political economy, and an angry flyer someone would pass you on the street.

Starting with the construction site and the physical building of houses, the book slowly builds and links more and more issues together: from gentrification and city politics to gender roles and identity politics, from subcontracting and speculation to union contracts and negotiation, from individual belief, suffering, and resistance to structural division, necessity, and instabil-ity. What starts as a look at housing broadens into a critique of capitalism as a whole. The text is accompanied by clean black-and-white illustrations that are mocking, beautiful, and bleak.

Praise:
"A thorough and easy-to-read analysis of the fight at the construction site and what the condi-tions are for the struggle in the city and for the land."
—Kämpa Tillsammans!

"Part illustrated guide to Marx, part analysis of the everyday consequences of producing and consuming housing as a commodity, and part revolutionary call to arms!"
—Aufheben

ON THE GROUND

AN ILLUSTRATED
ANECDOTAL HISTORY
OF THE SIXTIES
UNDERGROUND PRESS
IN THE U.S.

EDITED BY SEAN STEWART

On the Ground: An Illustrated Anecdotal History of the Sixties Underground Press in the U.S.
Edited by Sean Stewart
SKU: 978-I-60486-455-7
$20.00   224 pages

In four short years (I965–I969), the underground press grew from five small newspapers in as many cities in the U.S. to over 500 newspapers—with millions of readers—all over the world. Completely circumventing (and subverting) establishment media by utilizing their own news service and freely sharing content amongst each other, the underground press, at its height, became the unifying institution for the counterculture of the I960s.

Frustrated with the lack of any mainstream media criticism of the Vietnam War, empowered by the victories of the Civil Rights era, emboldened by the anti-colonial movements in the third world and with heads full of acid, a generation set out to change the world. The underground press was there documenting, participating in, and providing the resources that would guarantee the growth of this emergent youth culture. Combining bold visuals, innovative layouts, and eschewing any pretense toward objectivity, the newspapers were wildly diverse and wonderfully vibrant.

Neither meant to be an official nor comprehensive history, *On the Ground* focuses on the anecdotal detail that brings the history alive. Composed of stories told by the people involved with the production and distribution of the newspapers—John Sinclair, Art Kunkin, Paul Krassner, Emory Douglas, John Wilcock, Bill Ayers, Spain Rodriguez, Trina Robbins, Al Goldstein, Harvey Wasserman, and more—and featuring over 50 full-color scans taken from a broad range of newspapers—*Basta Ya, Berkeley Barb, Berkeley Tribe, Chicago Seed, Helix, It Ain't Me Babe, Los Angeles Free Press, Osawatomie, Rat Subterranean News, San Francisco Express Times, San Francisco Oracle, Screw: The Sex Review, The Black Panther, The East Village Other, The Realist*, and many more—the book provides a true window into the spirit of the times, giving the reader a feeling for the energy on the ground.

These are indisputably momentous times – the financial system is melting down globally and the Empire is stumbling. Now more than ever there is a vital need for radical ideas.

In the four years since its founding—and on a mere shoestring—PM Press has risen to the formidable challenge of publishing and distributing knowledge and entertainment for the struggles ahead. With over 175 releases to date, we have published an impressive and stimulating array of literature, art, music, politics, and culture. Using every available medium, we've succeeded in connecting those hungry for ideas and information to those putting them into practice.

Friends of PM allows you to directly help impact, amplify, and revitalize the discourse and actions of radical writers, filmmakers, and artists. It provides us with a stable foundation from which we can build upon our early successes and provides a much-needed subsidy for the materials that can't necessarily pay their own way. You can help make that happen —and receive every new title automatically delivered to your door once a month—by joining as a Friend of PM Press. And, we'll throw in a free T-Shirt when you sign up.

Here are your options:
• $25 a month: Get all books and pamphlets plus 50% discount on all webstore purchases
• $40 a month: Get all PM Press releases (including CDs and DVDs) plus 50% discount on all webstore purchases
• $100 a month: Superstar—Everything plus PM merchandise, free downloads, and 50% discount on all webstore purchases

For those who can't afford $25 or more a month, we're introducing Sustainer Rates at $15, $10 and $5. Sustainers get a free PM Press t-shirt and a 50% discount on all purchases from our website.

Your Visa or Mastercard will be billed once a month, until you tell us to stop. Or until our efforts succeed in bringing the revolution around. Or the financial meltdown of Capital makes plastic redundant. Whichever comes first.

PM Press was founded at the end of 2007 by a small collection of folks with decades of publishing, media, and organizing experience. PM Press co-conspirators have published and distributed hundreds of books, pamphlets, CDs, and DVDs. Members of PM have founded enduring book fairs, spearheaded victorious tenant organizing campaigns, and worked closely with bookstores, academic conferences, and even rock bands to deliver political and challenging ideas to all walks of life. We're old enough to know what we're doing and young enough to know what's at stake.

We seek to create radical and stimulating fiction and non-fiction books, pamphlets, t-shirts, visual and audio materials to entertain, educate and inspire you. We aim to distribute these through every available channel with every available technology— whether that means you are seeing anarchist classics at our bookfair stalls; reading our latest vegan cookbook at the café; downloading geeky fiction e-books; or digging new music and timely videos from our website.

PM Press is always on the lookout for talented and skilled volunteers, artists, activists and writers to work with. If you have a great idea for a project or can contribute in some way, please get in touch.

PM Press
PO Box 23912
Oakland CA 94623
510-658-3906
www.pmpress.org

CPSIA information can be obtained
at www.ICGtesting.com
Printed in the USA
LVHW052053071021
699864LV00004B/4